Letters to Bill

Letters to Bill

on University Administration

By

GEORGE LYNN CROSS

Foreword by

THEODORE M. HESBURGH, C.S.C.

UNIVERSITY OF OKLAHOMA PRESS : Norman

By George Lynn Cross

The World of Ideas: Essays on the Past and Future (with others; Norman, 1968)

Blacks in White Colleges: Oklahoma's Landmark Cases (Norman, 1975)

Presidents Can't Punt: The OU Football Tradition (Norman, 1977)

The University of Oklahoma and World War II (Norman, 1980)

Professors, Presidents, and Politicians: Civil Rights and the University of Oklahoma, 1890-1968 (Norman, 1981)

Letters to Bill: On University Administration (Norman, 1983)

Library of Congress Cataloging in Publication Data

Cross, George Lynn.
   Letters to Bill on university administration.

   Includes index.
   1. Universities and colleges—United States—Administration. 2. University of Oklahoma—Administration. 3. Cross, George Lynn. 4. University of Oklahoma—Presidents—Biography. I. Title.
LB2341.C86   1983   378.73   83-47832

The paper in this book meets the guidelines for permanence and durability of the Committee on Production Guidelines for Book Longevity of the Council on Library Resources, Inc.

Contents

Foreword

BY THEODORE M. HESBURGH, C.S.C.

George Lynn Cross, botanist and former collegiate football player, joined the faculty of the University of Oklahoma as an assistant professor in 1934. Promotions took him through the professorial ranks to the headship of his department and, during World War II, to the dual appointments of acting dean of the Graduate College and acting director of the University of Oklahoma Research Institute. In late 1943 the acting presidency of his institution was added to his responsibilities, and in mid-1944 he became the seventh president of the university. This gamut of faculty and administrative experiences gave him ample opportunity to observe university operations from a variety of perspectives, and provided a basis upon which a philosophy of university management would be developed. His *Letters to Bill* summarize that philosophy.

I first met President Cross during the fall of 1952, when he, Mrs. Cross, and their small son Bill came to South Bend to see a Notre Dame-Oklahoma football game as travel guests of a Notre Dame alumnus living in Tulsa, Oklahoma. We had dinner together on the evenings preceding and following the football game, and of course, we sat together during the game. We had time to discuss many matters having to do with the administration of higher education.

At that time, President Cross was greatly concerned about the administration of intercollegiate athletics—especially the development of acceptable regulations concerning the control of financial aid to athletes and ensuring that such aid was controlled by the institutions. The rules of his conference and the National Collegiate Athletic Association provided that an athlete could receive aid only in the form of a job with an hourly rate no greater than that paid to non-athletes. President Cross knew that there were widespread violations of this regulation in his institution and others. He knew that an athlete could not work enough hours to pay his way through school, spend enough hours in practice to perform creditably, and still find time for enough study to remain eligible for participation. The result was that many athletic departments provided jobs for athletes without requiring them to perform any services or that fans of the institution supplied them with funds in violation of the regulations. He thought that the situation tended to erode the ethics of all who were associated with athletic programs, but he was especially concerned with the impact on the young athletes, who knew that they were receiving illegal aid. In his letters he stresses the role of the university in helping students develop ethical and moral principles. Where, if not in a university, could one expect to find ethical behavior?

To illustrate his point, President Cross initiated and led a move in his conference to establish more reasonable regulations for athletic aid. He gradually persuaded presidents of other institutions in his conference to join in a movement, which finally established athletic scholarships as they exist today—board and room, tuition, books, and a small amount of money for incidental expenses. The plan was finally approved by the NCAA. This system of aid, while it by no means solved completely the problems of illegal aid to athletes, was a very positive step forward.

But President Cross was also heavily involved with many problems of higher education that were not related to athletics. He spent much time coping with racial desegregation in his institution, assuring civil rights for university employees, faculty participation in the formation of university policy, and, especially, the proper function of administration in university operations. His experiences led him to stress that the basic components of a university are students, faculty, and library; he maintains that the central administration is the capstone of several strata of service components whose basic responsibility is to provide an environment favorable for scholarly effort. In so doing, he does not deny the administration the right to make suggestions concerning academic affairs, but he insists that such suggestions must be presented to those affected for consideration and recommendation.

His *Letters to Bill,* through anecdotes and accounts of his own problems in relation to Bill's fictional ones, provide a total philosophy of dealing with university administration— including relations with students, faculty, governing boards, alumni, legislatures and news media. It is a philosophy that he not only advocates but exemplifies. The book should be useful not only to college and university presidents but to all readers interested in gaining a better understanding of what higher education is all about. I commend it to one and all.

Preface

Since my retirement from the presidency of the University of Oklahoma in 1968, I have been involved part time in the preparation of informal historical accounts of the major issues and events of my tenure as president. Included were desegregation of higher education; World War II and its impact on higher education, especially at the University of Oklahoma; the problems associated with the development of a super-successful football program; and the evolution of concepts and procedures concerning civil rights for members of the University's academic community.

As I was working on these various projects, a friend suggested that I should write something concerning my philosophy of university administration. He pointed out that, after nearly twenty-five years' experience as a university president, I should have something worthwhile to suggest—something useful to other university administrators and also to those who try to evaluate the performance of university administrators.

I first gave scant attention to the suggestion. I could not think of anything that would be less interesting to potential readers than my ideas of how a university should be administered. Moreover, I reasoned, in some respects university administration has changed so markedly since my retirement that my views surely would be obsolete—only moderately significant as historical record. With rare exceptions modern university presidents and others are disinclined to look to the past for guidance of any kind, despite abundant evidence that we can go forward successfully only by knowing and understanding where we have been.

Later, while visiting with an editor of the University of

Oklahoma Press, the question of what I might write about in the future came up. I mentioned my friend's suggestion but dismissed it as implausible. The editor countered with the suggestion that, while a treatise on university administration as such might not be feasible, a project involving a different format might be worthwhile. She suggested a series of letters to a fictitious nephew who had become president of a fictitious state university with concerns similar to those of the University of Oklahoma during my tenure. Such letters, she pointed out, centering on my nephew's reported relations with his students, faculty, governing board, legislature, and general public, could be used to present, in successive segments, my ideas of university administration. In addition, the format would be sufficiently flexible to permit the use of interesting episodes of my own administrative experience to illustrate certain points.

After careful thought I decided that this approach might indeed be promising. Letters have been used effectively in literature to convey advice and ideas and to record interesting events. By way of example, Alan Valentine's *Fathers to Sons: Advice Without Consent,* an edition of authentic letters from the past, has substantial merit.[1] In the modern era Screwtape's letters to Wormwood demonstrate how a senior devil sought to pass on helpful suggestions to a junior devil concerning the art of temptation.[2] While I could not hope to approach the literary quality or persuasiveness that characterize Screwtape's efforts, perhaps I could produce something worthwhile. Moreover, I reasoned, while the role of the university president changes constantly, certain basic principles

[1] Alan Valentine, *Fathers to Sons: Advice Without Consent* (Norman: University of Oklahoma Press, 1963).
[2] C. S. Lewis, *The Screwtape Letters* (New York: Macmillan Publishing Co., 1961).

remain unchanged, and it could do no harm to affirm them. I decided to make the effort.

The choice of the name Bill for the recipient of the letters has no significance. Any resemblance to presidents of that name, present or in the past, is purely coincidental.

GEORGE LYNN CROSS

Norman, Oklahoma

Letters to Bill

The Presidency in Perspective

June 28

Dear Bill,

Your letter saying that you will soon change your status from professor to president of your university did not come as a surprise; I had already received word through the news media. My first reaction was to recall a quotation from the writings of John Dryden: "'Tis fate that flings the dice, and in the fling, does of kings peasants make and peasants kings." But I dismissed the thought speedily; if there is anything that a president is not, or should not be, it is a king. And certainly faculty members are not peasants, though they sometimes allege that they are treated as such.

I have mixed emotions about your situation, because I know from personal experience that there likely will be times in the future when you will wonder whether the change represented a promotion or a demotion. The presidency of a sizable state university carries with it impressive responsibilities usually not clearly understood by those who accept the appointments. If this were not true, there would be far fewer candidates for the top administrative posts in the country's colleges and universities.

Nevertheless, I congratulate you sincerely, not so much because I think you are improving your status in the academic world as because the governing board of your institution thought you were the man for the job. This is a very great compliment, assuming, of course, that the members of your board have discriminating judgment, an assumption that is not always valid.

I am flattered by your thought that I might be a source of occasional helpful advice as you make the change and in the future. Your situation does indeed parallel my own, and if I learned anything during my long tenure as president of the University of Oklahoma, I'll be more than happy to share it with you. I could scarcely do less for a member of the Cross clan.

The first thing you need to do is place yourself and the job you will hold in proper perspective. This will not be easy, and your initial impressions are likely to change as the years pass. I recall remarks made by Robert Maynard Hutchins at a trustee-faculty dinner at the University of Chicago in 1944, an event staged in recognition of his fifteenth anniversary as president of the school. While at the lectern, Hutchins said that with the passing of years he had gradually realized that

> the nearest analogue to a university president who has served fifteen years is a champion flagpole sitter. The remarkable thing about him is not what he has done, but that he has done it so long. And you sometimes wonder why he should want to do it at all. The fact is that as a university president proceeds up to and beyond the fifteen year mark, his loss of knowledge, accompanied by his loss of health, hair, teeth, appetite, character, figure, and friends, becomes nothing short of sensational.

I was just getting started as president of OU at the time, and I regarded Hutchins's remarks as a humorous minimization of his brilliant record at Chicago. Later I would realize that there was more than a trace of truth in what he said.

In those days no professional training had been designed for prospective college presidents. Charles Dollard, president of the Carnegie Corporation of New York, commented on this back in the 1940s. In reflecting on what might be done, he suggested that a suitable academic background for a university president should include courses and experience in "banking and diplomacy, door-to-door selling, public relations, juvenile delinquency, and, for good measure, a little training in psychiatry."

Dollard's tongue-in-cheek proposal would produce an amazingly diverse curriculum, though not more diverse than the responsibilities of a university president. But while a president does indeed have interesting and varied responsibilities, he usually has little to do directly with the main business of the university, which is scholarship. This may have led Walter A. Jessup, president of the Carnegie Corporation for the Advancement of Teaching, to stress the personal characteristics of a university's chief administrator, rather than his academic background. Jessup said:

> The president must be all things to all men. He must be a man who will charm the prospective donor, who will delight the student with his youthfulness, who will have wisdom and experience to lead the faculty to make decisions with unanimity, who will take full responsibility for a winning football team, who will say nothing to outrage either the "stand patter" or the "new dealer," at the same time standing four square on all things. He ought also to be a man who is religious enough to suit the fundamentalists but sufficiently worldly not to outrage the bibulous alumni. Truly, such a man is a white blackbird.

Jessup, it is reported, regarded a university presidency as such a high-risk occupation that on occasion he advised some of his young friends not to become interested in the administration of higher education.

There were times during my nearly twenty-five-year tenure at OU that I agreed with Jessup. As the years went by, I realized increasingly that enjoyment of the prestige and perquisites related to the job was more than nullified by the endless frustrating problems and criticism that came almost daily to the president's office. I found it difficult to develop the patience suggested by Otis D. Coffman, one-time president of the University of Minnesota, who said, "A college president is like a big game hunter who spends 95% of his time swatting mosquitoes while remembering that he is where he is in order to get a shot at a moose." Sometime late in the first decade of my presidency, I gazed somberly at a motto on my desk that read, "Count that day lost when you don't get hell for something." But I then brightened at the thought that I had not lost a single day in more than eight years.

In the intervening years colleges of education throughout the country have developed curricula for would-be educational administrators at all levels, including university presidents. However, I am skeptical that they can be effective. I find myself in agreement with Harold W. Stoke, former president of Louisiana State University, who wrote in his excellent book *The American College President* (page 20) that a university presidency involves several paradoxes: those who enjoy it are not likely to be very successful, and those who are successful are not likely to be happy. Stoke suggests that the explanation is hidden somewhere in the philosophy of power: "Those who enjoy exercising power shouldn't have it, and those who should exercise it are not likely to enjoy it."

I realize that this letter is getting long, and, while I have some other comments, I'll send them along later. There will be plenty of time, inasmuch as you do not take over your new duties for several weeks.

My love to Diane and the children.

Affectionately,

Central Administration—
A Service Department

Dear Bill,

I am glad that you found my letter of June 28 interesting, if not particularly reassuring. I should perhaps point out that this is likely to characterize the bulk of your future professional life—much of interest but very little of reassurance.

Today I want to probe a bit deeper into my suggestion that your first effort should be to place yourself and the job you will hold in proper perspective. At the moment I suspect that you may be somewhat overimpressed with your own importance in this changing situation. I know that this was true of me back in December, 1943, when I was named acting president of the University of Oklahoma. It is usually difficult for an individual to realize that being selected to fill an important position does not increase his own importance. It merely provides an opportunity for him to achieve importance through sustained effective effort. Certainly your new job is one of prestige and influence, but you will have to earn these characteristics for yourself; they don't come with the job. I suggest that you start the effort by giving careful thought to the relationship of the administration of the university to the rest of the institution.

The basic concern of a university, of course, is knowledge—its discovery and preservation (research and publication), dissemination (classroom and laboratory activities), and use (interpretation and synthesis of what has been learned). From this it follows that the faculty must be considered the most important element of the institution. The faculty and

7

the library determine the quality of the educational effort; they are, in effect, the university. It is surprising that these facts, which seem to be very obvious, are frequently overlooked by presidents and others involved with university administration, including governing boards.

The central administration of a university, as I see it, should be considered the upper echelon of a series of service departments. As the service capstone of the institution, it has the responsibility of seeing that the other service departments maintain a campus climate in which the basic functions mentioned above can be performed by the faculty with maximum effectiveness and minimum interference. As Herman B. Wells, the enormously successful president of the University of Indiana for many years, once said: "Administration is not an end unto itself and exists only to further the academic enterprise. It follows, therefore, that the least administration possible is the best." In other words, your new job should never be considered an end in itself, but only a means to an end.

Unfortunately, this view is not widely held by those who control the destiny of higher education. In many, perhaps most, of the country's colleges and universities administration is regarded as the most important part of the campus program. This is reflected in the salary differential between faculty members and administrative officials and a burgeoning of administrative structures that has produced higher educational bureaucracies rivaling those of the federal government.

The idea of university administration as a service department, however, is widely approved by faculties. On occasions I have heard faculty members compare the central administration of their institution with the maintenance staff of the physical plant and grounds—frequently an unfavorable

8

comparison. This probably stems from the plethora of assistant deans, deans, assistant vice-presidents, vice-presidents, assistant provosts, provosts, and assistants to the president through which a frustrated department chairman must go in dealing with the administration.

What I am trying to advise you, I suppose, is not to overindulge in building your administrative organization as you take over the new job. You will need far fewer people than you originally thought and probably far fewer than you will inherit from your predecessor. If overstaffing turns out to be a problem, you can solve it by attrition—by consolidating functions and not filling vacancies. If you can create an impression of austerity in your administrative operations, seemingly giving financial preference to the academic programs, yet get your job done in reasonable fashion, you will be surprised by the faculty support that will come your way.

You will have occasional meetings with your vice-presidents and other administrative subordinates. Be sure that these meetings are carefully structured and disciplined. Do not permit them to become involved with matters of secondary and tertiary importance that should be delegated to individual vice-presidents or deans. Much time can be wasted in such meetings, because those in attendance are likely to feel that they should impress the president with their grasp of the situation. On the other hand, do not do too much talking yourself. Never give your own opinion on any matter until you have heard the opinions of others. If you do, you will receive no input, because relatively few subordinates will express views differing from those of their superiors. If you find such in your organization, cherish them! In all meetings the theme should be positive—place the emphasis on finding out how something can be done rather than why it cannot be done. Herman Wells, whom I mentioned earlier, once said, "The central administration should always be a source of inspiration and expedition, rather than a bottleneck practiced in the art of saying 'No.'"

That's it for today. I'll save further thoughts for later.

Affectionately,

P.S. Always remember that, when stress develops in a meeting, a calm, rational, positive attitude by the president will tend to keep others from overreacting.

On Faculty Relations

Dear Bill,

I am sorry that my emphasis on the importance of the faculty gave you the impression that I denigrate, or at least discount to some extent, the importance of the university president. I certainly did not intend to imply this. I mentioned that the central administration of an institution has the responsibility of maintaining a campus climate favorable for faculty effort. That is of the utmost importance, because it determines the success of what goes on in the classrooms and laboratories. Much more is involved here than merely providing an adequate physical plant with well-equipped facilities and proper financing of projects, important as those are. I will try to explain what I have in mind.

Like other public universities, your institution is organized into colleges, schools, departments, and a variety of services and auxiliary enterprises not directly related to classroom instruction. Looking back through history, from the time of Plato's Academy through the Middle Ages, with the developments at Salerno, Bologna, Paris, Oxford, and Cambridge, we can see that this specialization and segmentation came from an increasing understanding of the benefits that could come to society from higher education, an understanding that produced an increasing demand for services. The evolution of the modern university is splendidly discussed by Clark Kerr, former president of the University of California, in his book *The Uses of the University.* Although published in 1963, the book is still well worth reading, and I suggest that you get a copy. The evolutionary process that Kerr describes, with its proliferation of campus communities,

11

and even campuses, was inevitable, but the resulting segmentation has made institutional management much more difficult. The chief administrator is likely to be not an intellectual giant like William Rainey Harper or Nicholas Murray Butler but rather an individual gifted as a mediator, coordinator, and initiator. In some cases it would appear that presidents have been hired because of unique special abilities to do certain things—to achieve specific goals, such as changing the image of a university—without expectation that they will actually be a part of the institution. After achieving the goals, they pass on to other things.

The abilities to mediate and to coordinate are of great importance, because each of the many departments and other units of a modern university tends to operate in isolation, and even in competition. Each is inclined to pursue its own interests without regard to what is going on elsewhere. Under these conditions dissension and polarization frequently develop. There is much need to mediate and coordinate the many segments, to the end that the institution will make a unified, rather than piecemeal, contribution to the society it serves.

The president's responsibilities do not end with mediation and coordination, however. Although increasingly removed from the academic scene by these activities—and the inevitable fund-raising efforts, he must sometimes be innovative and use his initiative in the development of his institution. He should feel free to propose new programs or the modification of existing ones. In most instances he will need to work through the faculty senate in getting things done. Impatient presidents are tempted to govern by fiat, but such methods usually do not work out well in the long run. Over a period of time a faculty can find countless ways to demonstrate why action taken by executive order was unwise. It is one thing to get something started and quite another to keep it going.

I must add that in any attempt to exert influence on campus affairs, either directly or through his staff, the president must use extreme tact and delicacy in presenting his ideas if they are to find acceptance. He should realize that he is, at best, only a generalist dealing with sometimes temperamental specialists, and frequently the faculty will not rate him high even as a generalist.

Almost immediately after becoming president of OU, I discovered that my ideas concerning academic affairs were regarded warily by members of the faculty, or even ignored completely. I soon decided that if I wanted to exert influence in bringing about changes in campus procedures or policies I would have to operate indirectly and make occasional use of subterfuge. When I had an idea I thought worthwhile, I would invite some prominent member of the Faculty Senate to have coffee with me. After asking and receiving his advice concerning some matter, I would turn the conversation to a casual discussion of campus affairs. Then at what seemed to be the proper time I would present the idea as if it had occurred to me at the moment and follow with a series of questions designed to cause my coffee companion to come to think that my idea was at least partly his own. This was never particularly difficult, because faculty members are inclined to be flattered when their advice is sought by the president; being asked for advice puts them in a receptive mood.

As soon as my companion had developed some enthusiasm for the proposal, I would seem to lose interest in the matter, suggesting that, of course, there would be no way of getting the approval of the Faculty Senate. This challenge to my friend's influence in the Senate usually produced results.

Almost certainly he would present the proposal to the Senate at the next meeting. When the journal of the Senate appeared, I would note that the proposal had been presented and had been referred to a committee for study and recommendation.

My next step would be to find some member of the committee and, during casual discussion, express mild skepticism about the proposal. I knew that my skepticism would be reported at the next meeting of the committee and almost surely would bring support for the proposal and a favorable report to the Senate. Then, when the Senate's recommendation for action reached my office, I would give approval on a trial basis—to see how things worked out. Knowledge that action taken by the Senate had been approved by a cautious president, but only on a trial basis, almost always produced enough faculty support to ensure that the new policy or procedure would be successful.

Of course, I did not use this method on every occasion in dealing with the Senate, but I did find it useful several times during my nearly twenty-five years as president of OU.

You should bear in mind that, while an ideal situation might be one in which the faculty would be so organized as to have control of the academic activities of a university and a voice in all matters, that ideal is seldom achieved. During times of highly centralized administration, faculties are inclined to strive for a greater voice in institutional affairs. Upon achieving influence in university governance, however, they are likely to become lax in exercising it.

As I look back through the years, it occurs to me that faculty influence has ebbed and flowed, somewhat in wave action, in several universities with which I am acquainted. Faculty members' participation reached a zenith following World War II and throughout the 1950s, but their influence declined sharply during the 1960s, when they seemed to become indifferent to institutional affairs. This may have been due to the appearance on the scene of younger faculty members who had never experienced authoritarianism in higher education and were inclined to neglect committee assignments on the grounds that the issues involved were really the responsibility of the administration.

During the 1970s the erosion of faculty influence became a matter of concern to the American Association of University Professors, and various ways of regaining influence have been proposed from time to time. Such efforts are likely to be only partly successful. The trend, I think, is toward tight central administration of all university matters except those pertaining to the academic programs. While I think this may not be a good thing, it seems inevitable. With greatly improved faculty salaries—dramatic improvement at the University of Oklahoma, for instance—members are likely to be content with their lot, disinclined to crusade for participation in university affairs.

Needless to say, if I were in your position, I would encourage faculty participation in all university planning. Those involved in the planning of any venture are much more likely to help it succeed.

Glancing back at the paragraphs above, I think it possible that I may have exaggerated somewhat the difficulty a university president has in dealing with his faculty. While the gamut of human characteristics will likely be found in any group the size of your faculty, on the whole I think you will find them to be reasonable people. If you treat them as colleagues rather than employees, seek the senate's advice on most matters—whether or not you follow it—and be honest and impartial in dealing with everyone, you should get along well.

Affectionately,

The President's Wife

Dear Bill,

Diane is rightly concerned about possible changes in her way of life when you assume the presidency: A president's wife plays an important role in university affairs—so important, in fact, that when the OU regents were looking for a president before my appointment they stressed the importance of the wife and spoke of the need to make a "team appointment." In those days the president's wife was expected to play an important role in campus and public relations. She was the first lady and hostess of the institution. Lloyd Noble, an influential OU regent, stated flatly that the qualifications of the candidate's wife were as important as those of the candidate. Of course, time has changed this kind of thinking, and the president's wife is no longer expected to make the institution her sole, or even primary, interest. The women's-rights movement probably had much to do with this change in attitude.

However, despite the fact that wives are now largely accepted as individuals entitled to seek their own fulfillment independent of their husbands, the wife of a university president cannot escape being spotlighted frequently as such, and on occasion she will be expected to function as a gracious adjunct to the presidency. Moreover, I know from experience that a mutually rewarding cooperative relationship can be worked out. I think your Aunt Cleo would agree that this is so.

Of course, as I look back fifty-five years into the past, I am struck by the fact that our relationship, from the beginning, seemed almost designed to promote team effort. Our romance, which developed during the mid-1920s when we were students at South Dakota State College, was strongly opposed by Cleo's mother and sister. During the summer of 1926 they decided that Cleo should transfer to the University of Minnesota for her junior and senior years. That should put an end to the nonsense, because I was scheduled to begin a master's program at South Dakota State College that fall.

Word of this disastrous family maneuver reached me at the University of Chicago, where I was enrolled for the summer session. Cleo was sorry, she said in her letter, but she was simply unable to withstand the pressure from her mother and sister.

I was unable to launch a counteroffensive immediately because, in addition to my academic program, my own mother's illness, and finally death, in the early autumn of 1926 brought many cares.

But I was the proud owner of a Model-T Ford coupé, which my mother, doubtless with much juggling of family finances, had given me for graduation the preceding spring. I took off in the little vehicle at 4:30 on the morning of October 27 and arrived at Minneapolis in midafternoon. Cleo and I were married the next day, without having given serious consideration to how we would live on the eighty dollars a month I received for teaching a course at South Dakota State College while I worked for my master's degree. But our act of defiance in the face of such odds placed squarely upon us the responsibility for seeing that things worked out well.

I received my master's degree in the spring of 1927 and then taught bacteriology the following year so that Cleo could complete the requirements for a bachelor of science.

In the meantime I had received a scholarship from the University of Chicago sufficient to pay my tuition while I worked for the Ph.D. there. Our family assets totaled about $750—a rather bleak economic prospect. Things might work out, but only if Cleo could find a job.

I left for Chicago in early June, 1928, leaving Cleo to spend a week or so with her mother, hoping that the family breach caused by our marriage could finally be healed completely. There had been some progress along this line during the past two years, but trips to her mother's home had not been pleasant experiences—at least not for me.

Cleo arrived in Chicago by train a week or so later, reached the campus at 11:00 A.M., and hurried to the placement bureau in search of a job. She went to work as assistant cashier in the football ticket office at 1:00 P.M. that afternoon. The future looked bright. Parenthetically I might add that that was the last year that Chicago played big-time football. Cleo insists that she had nothing to do with its demise.

After the ticket job ended, Cleo became first a file clerk and then receptionist in the university's placement bureau. Her salary paid all our living expenses. While I was properly appreciative of this contribution, it was her activities as a receptionist that first made me aware of her extraordinary potential as a member of the "team."

Because I was scheduled to receive my doctorate in December, 1929, I registered with the placement bureau in the fall of that year. A few weeks later I received a telephone call from the president of Wittenberg College, in Springfield, Ohio. He said that he was looking for a botanist to add to his faculty the following year and that my name had been suggested by the head of the botany department at Chicago. Could I have dinner with him at the Stephens Hotel that evening? I quickly agreed.

The same morning Cleo also received a call from Wittenberg's president. He asked whether she could send a file on

18

George L. Cross, with whom he would have dinner that evening. She agreed to send the papers by special messenger. The president then asked, "Do you happen to know this young man?" Cleo acknowledged an acquaintanceship. The president asked whether she could tell him anything about his prospect that might be helpful. Cleo said, "I'm sorry that I must disqualify myself. He is my husband." The president then invited her to come with me to dinner that evening.

After a good dinner and an hour or so of pleasant talk, the president offered me a job as professor of botany and quickly followed with an offer of a half-time job for Cleo if she would be willing to organize a placement bureau at his college. We expressed proper appreciation and promised the president that we would let him know within the next few days.

Of course, you know that we did not go to Wittenberg. When we got back to our apartment that evening, after a somewhat euphoric ride on the elevated train that connects the Chicago Loop with 63d Street, we found a note in our mailbox from E. J. Kraus, head of the Department of Botany at Chicago. The note said that the dean of the College of Arts and Sciences in the University of South Dakota had telephoned him that day. He was at the Stephens Hotel and was looking for a botanist to fill a vacancy at South Dakota effective in the fall of 1930. The dean wanted me to call him at the hotel.

That led to another dinner at the Stephens Hotel and a position at South Dakota. While the dean did not offer Cleo a job, it seemed to me that he was more interested in talking with her that evening than in interviewing me.

After four years at the University of South Dakota we moved to the University of Oklahoma. The first Saturday night in Norman we went to a movie at the Sooner Theater, on Main Street. As we were leaving the theater, we passed a rather small man with a mustache. His hat was pulled down close to his eyes. Cleo clutched my arm and whispered, "I know that man. He was registered at the placement bureau at the University of Chicago. His name is Royden Danger-field, and he teaches political science." Amazed by this feat of memory, I asked her how she could possibly recall the name of someone she had met only once or twice, after a lapse of more than four years. She explained that when she became receptionist at the placement bureau the director had stressed the need to remember names—especially names of potential employers of Chicago graduates. Jobs were not plentiful, and a talent scout might be put in a much more receptive frame of mind if he heard his name called when he entered the office. Cleo said that she had taken the director's admonition very seriously.

I interpreted this ingenuous explanation as an attempt to be humorous, but I became very thoughtful a couple of weeks later when, at a faculty reception, Cleo spotted a woman across the room and remarked "That is Dora McFarland. She used to come to the placement bureau at the University of Chicago." A few minutes later she said, "See that man at the end of the table? His name is Lowry Doran. He was registered at the placement bureau, too."

Even so, I did not become fully aware of Cleo's talent for remembering names until some time later, a few weeks after I was named acting president of OU. We were attend-ing an alumni meeting in Muskogee. There was an excep-tionally good turnout that evening—between eighty and ninety couples, as I recall. It occurred to me that this would be a good time to test her ability to recall names, and I suggested a competition for the two of us. After meeting the alumni in a receiving line, we would see who could remember the most names at evening's end. As we shook hands with the departing couples, she was able to recall the names of all but four. Despite the best concentration I could summon, I was able to recall less than a fourth of the names.

After my status was changed from acting president to president, each fall we held an evening reception for the new women students on campus—freshmen and transfers from other institutions. Every year seven hundred to a thousand young women attended the three-hour reception. During one of these social events it dawned on me why Cleo could remember names better than I could. After shaking hands with thirty-five or forty students, I found myself losing interest in the occasion and paying little attention to their names. Cleo, on the other hand, was just as interested in the last girl to appear as she was in the first. Proof of this was provided one May when she was serving as hostess to a group of mothers participating in the University's Mother's Day activities. Upon being introduced to one mother, she remarked, "Oh, yes, I met your freshman daughter last fall. You're from Ponca City, aren't you?" The freshman daughter had appeared at the reception the preceding September.

Needless to say, I soon found it expedient to stay close to Cleo when we paid alumni groups in the state a second visit. She would remember the *names* of more alumni than I could remember having *seen.* Salty Captain Mike Parrish, who presided over the closing of the naval base in Norman after World War II, was fond of saying that she was "the best damned name caller I ever knew."

I think that a university president's wife is more likely to enjoy her role if she can come to regard it as a career in itself—not merely supportive of her husband's. Cleo considered herself the University's hostess, and she planned her program to a large extent independently of other University functions. She enjoyed entertaining and always personally prepared at least one dish for the dinners we gave in the president's home. When, during one of our early years, she decided that she wanted to invite all the international students, about six hundred of them, to dinner at the president's house, I was appalled. But things went very well that Sunday evening; more than five hundred students, with well-filled plates, ate at three levels in the house, seated on chairs, the stairs, and the floor.

Cleo did not permit herself to be restricted in any way by university activities. She wanted three children, not only two, and, as you know, Braden was born in the third year of my presidency. She liked to work with young people, and she was very active in Campfire. She became a member of the Campfire national board, and was scheduled to become president but decided against the latter responsibility, because it would involve extensive traveling for a year, and she did not want to be away from her family. Somehow she found time for a great variety of hobbies—knitting and various other kinds of needlework, china painting, and even recaning antique chairs that she had been collecting.

Knowing Diane as I do, I am sure that she will be able to cope with her new responsibilities well. But she will do best if she comes to think of her activities as a career of her own. The supportive role simply does not appeal to some women—perhaps a great many. There was an example of this, which, incidentally, involved a member of Cleo's family.

The husband of a cousin of Cleo's became president of a western state university. Cleo's cousin was a very competent woman and a strong believer in women's rights. She found life as a university president's wife so frustrating that after a couple of years she sued for divorce. That, of course, was an extreme case which probably could have been avoided by some frank discussions and planning before the couple moved into the president's home. It is also possible, of course, that the presidency simply made untenable an already strained family situation. One never knows about these things.

I am sure that Diane will get along very well. A visit with Cleo might help her, and I am hoping that the two of you can spend a few days with us before you take office. Why not include Norman on your itinerary for vacation in August? We would be pleased to have you.

Affectionately,

The President's Children

Dear Bill,

This can be regarded as a sort of postscript to my last letter. After mailing the perhaps too complete account of the problems of a university president's wife, it occurred to me that I had forgotten to discuss the effects of the presidency on the children. My firsthand experience with the latter gives me confidence to write of it with some assurance.

As you will recall, Cleo and I had two of our three children, Mary-Lynn and Bill, when we moved into the big house just north of the campus. (Braden was born a couple of years later, the only child, I believe, to be born to a president of OU in office.) Mary-Lynn, aged thirteen, was pleased by the move, but Bill, who was eight, was very much disappointed with the new neighborhood. There were no children within several blocks of the house, and Bill wondered why, if we had to move, it should be to such a poor location.

The children attended the University School (a laboratory school for the College of Education) without incident. During the next two or three years Bill adjusted to the new environment rather too rapidly. A somewhat brash and adventuresome youngster, he was reported to be boasting that he had been on top of all the buildings on the campus except the Administration Building. He then decided to explore the utility tunnel system beneath the campus. That led to a misadventure that caused some consternation to his parents, the campus police, and the women students living in Cate Center. Bill managed to pry the lid off a manhole and enter the tunnel late in the afternoon. After wandering around for a while and making a few turns, however, he became lost and could not find his way back to his entrance point. Hours later he emerged in the basement at Cate Center, where, after he went upstairs to try to get out, some partially clad coeds reported his presence to the campus police. Understandably embarrassed, he refused to identify himself, and it was some time before he was recognized and returned to where he belonged.

Bill had a penchant for getting involved with interesting situations. During the last years of World War II, when the university had several specialized training programs for the armed forces—both Army and Navy—soldiers and sailors in uniform were conspicuous on the campus. One day Cleo found a considerable sum of money in his room—in nickles, dimes, and quarters—rather more than his biweekly allowance could justify. There was immediate concern that he might have taken the money, concern accentuated by his evasiveness in supplying an explanation. Finally, after the exertion of more pressure than we usually used, he said that one day as he was walking behind a group of Army trainees it occurred to him to say, "The Army's here to win the war, but what the hell's the Navy for?" This brought laughter and a few coins from the group. He then decided that a more extensive use of the maneuver might be profitable. He would watch for groups of trainees on the campus and adjust his remark—using the words "Army" or "Navy" as might fit the situation. By this means over a period of time he had accumulated the money found in his room.

When Mary-Lynn graduated from high school, we decided that she should not enter the University of Oklahoma, but attend Monticello, in Alton, Illinois, a two-year college for women. The decision was based on the thought that at OU she would have difficulty being considered a person in her own right, rather than the daughter of the president of the University. After attending Monticello for a year, however, she decided to transfer to OU, where opportunities to study voice were better. She got along well after the transfer, and Eva Turner, the great English soprano, who was in residence at OU as visiting professor of voice, encouraged her to make an operatic career her objective. She was tempted for a time but finally decided to marry and rear a family.

When Bill graduated from high school, he was quite firm in announcing his desire to attend OU. But after his freshman year he decided to get his required military service out of the way and enlisted in the Navy for two years. After his discharge, he attended Phillips University, at Enid, Oklahoma, where he made an excellent academic record.

When Braden reached college age, Cleo and I were determined that he should go elsewhere for his higher education—perhaps Dartmouth, Oberlin, or Vanderbilt. But we were unable to convince him. When I told him that it would be a great mistake for him to enroll in the university of which his father was president, he wanted to know why. I explained carefully that his teachers and other associates in most instances would treat him not as an individual in his own right but as the president's son. They would likely either make things too easy for him in the hope of incurring the goodwill of his father or take the position that "just because he's the president's son he can't get by with anything." I suggested also that occasional criticism of his father by other students might bother him.

Braden listened patiently to my argument and then commented: "I don't see it that way. If I attend the University of Oklahoma, I will have my job and you will have yours. If you don't meddle with mine and I don't meddle with yours, there should be no problem." His persuasive logic prevailed, and he attended the University, including Medical

School, seemingly almost incognito. There were several other students named Cross in attendance at that time, and I had the impression that no one bothered to find out which, if any, were related to the president.

While my own experience would indicate that a president's daughter or son can attend his institution without undesirable effects, I nevertheless still have the feeling that it would be better for the president's children to go elsewhere. Of course, youngsters vary in their abilities to cope with such situations. Those unduly impressed with the importance of their father's position are likely to have problems. At the other extreme, those who are retiring and sensitive are likely to be affected adversely when they hear their father criticized.

Your oldest, of course, Michelle, was already in her freshman year at your university when you were named to the presidency. With this good start, she is likely to do well.

I am afraid this has been a rather long postscript; I hope you will find something helpful in it.

Affectionately,

The Governing Board

September 10

Dear Bill,

I enjoyed your account of your adventures during the first three weeks of your presidency, especially the problem that developed at the first monthly session with your board of regents. From well-remembered experience, I can understand your feelings of uncertainty during the first two or three days in office. When I went to my office that first day so many years ago, I recall similar uneasy moments. I didn't know how to signal my secretary in an adjoining room, and I couldn't figure out how to use the telephone equipment, a box with a slanting top and several levers. A kindly member of my predecessor's staff, who had served as secretary of the Board of Regents for many years, helped me learn my way around. My discomfiture was increased by the fact that, with the exception of the dean of the College of Law, all the deans of the university family were several years older than I. I suspected that the deans would resent having a much younger man intruding into the affairs of their schools and colleges. I was right. But enough of that for the moment; perhaps we'll have an opportunity to talk about deans sometime in the future.

As I recall, your governing board consists of seven members who serve staggered terms of seven years. The members are appointed by the governor, confirmed by the state senate, and, because they are a constitutional body, can be relatively free from political interference. This is a favorable plan for university governance, quite like that of the University of Oklahoma. But as I discovered at OU several years ago, and you are discovering now, a good plan for governance

28

does not necessarily mean that there will be good governance. The quality of the individuals involved in the plan is much more important than the plan itself. I believe it was Alexander Pope who said, "On forms of government let fools protest; What's best administered is best." I may be wrong, but it sounds like Pope.

To be successful, the president of a state university must learn to get along reasonably well with many diverse groups of people—students, faculty, regents, alumni, parents of students, legislators and other politicians, and various state organizations. Good relations with all are desirable, but by far the most important are the members of the governing board. The president serves at their will; he does not have tenure as chief executive officer of his institution, though he may have tenure as a professor in some department during his presidency.

Now, with reference to your problem, you should remember that the regent who was annoyingly insistent in suggesting that he knew exactly the right person to fill the vacancy created by the resignation of your director of housing, was a new appointee to the board, attending his second meeting. He did not yet understand the relationship that should exist between a governing board and its executive officer. You should not be too concerned about this; rather you should be reassured by the fact that his fellow members gave little or no support to his proposal.

Early in my career as president of OU, I found that newly appointed regents almost invariably had serious misconceptions concerning the structure and management of the institution. Almost without exception they had the impression that the institution was very like a business or industrial corporation and should be operated as such. They seemed to believe that competence to make decisions was concentrated in the upper level of institutional organization and that decisions originating there could be passed down to the workers (that is, the faculty) for implementation. They failed to realize that, while in a corporation intellectual competence may be concentrated in administrators, the reverse is true in a good university. In trying to explain this difference to new regents, I occasionally compared the university to a large medical center or hospital, whose top administrator would never presume to tell a doctor how to treat a patient but would concern himself only with providing adequate facilities for treatment. Like the superintendent of a medical center, a university president presides over professional personnel, not over workers in a factory.

While some new regents were slow to accept this concept, the fact that only one new one normally appeared on the board each year gave me time for an educational program. I would invite the new appointee to come to the campus for a visit, usually a couple of days and a night, to explore briefly the structure of the institution and learn something of its procedures. I would stress that, to ensure smooth operation, the president's recommendations to the board should almost always be related to advice received from the faculty and that no proposal initiated in a board meeting should be enacted without giving the segment of the university involved a chance to react. In a tactful way I would try to put across the idea that a regent should never try to tell the president what to recommend, but only approve or disapprove his recommendations and, in the latter event, perhaps make suggestions for his consideration. With a very few minor exceptions things worked out very well for me. Of course, I had a remarkably fine board my first year in office—including the head of a large corporation, the chief legal counsel of Oklahoma's largest oil company, two other lawyers, a physician, a newspaper publisher, and a small-town businessman. I did not have the problem of dealing with a new appointee during my first year, the regent whose term expired that spring was reappointed—a big help.

I should stress that members of your governing board need careful and continuous cultivation as a group and individually. However, in dealing with them as individuals, be careful to treat them impartially. You may be tempted to communicate more frequently with one or more outstanding members than with the others; but if you do, certain members of your board may feel excluded, and a polarized situation could develop. It is of the utmost importance that all problems of the university should be addressed by the governing board as a group, not by individual members or segments of the group. Of course, this does not apply to the chairman of the board, with whom you will exchange frequent correspondence and have other contacts. If your board sets up committees to study and make recommendations concerning specific areas of the institution, you will inevitably have frequent contacts with the committee chairmen.

Regents like to be entertained when they assemble for their meetings. A good dinner the evening before the meeting will usually put them in a good mood for the next day's work. And don't forget that regents have wives or husbands, some of whom may want to accompany their spouses to the sessions. Make careful plans for the entertainment of spouses—plans designed to ensure that they will be favorably impressed by what is going on at the institution. A regent's spouse can be a valuable ally of the president.

But enough about regents for the moment. Let me know, from time to time, how you are getting along with your board. I will always be interested.

Affectionately,

Relations with the State Legislature

September 25

Dear Bill,

I was interested in your report of your encounter with the state senator. You must expect an occasional experience of this kind. Political pressure is part of the price that one pays for being president of a state university. While state colleges and universities are now better insulated from political pressures than they were in my time, the political implications of the president's job are still very much with us.

Within a few weeks after I was named acting president of the University of Oklahoma, I had an experience similar to the one you described. The director of the university's radio station resigned, leaving a vacancy to be filled. Two or three days after his resignation was announced, a member of the legislature came to my office and announced that he knew just the right person to fill the vacancy. When I told him that I would be glad to have the person considered with other candidates for the position, he hinted that immediate action on my part might improve my chances of having the "acting" removed from my title. He assured me that he was on excellent terms with both the chairman of OU's Board of Regents and the governor. I knew, of course, that I could not do what he asked; the problem was how to explain the situation to him without making an enemy.

I finally explained carefully that, if I approved his request, I would have to do the same for any other member of the legislature who wanted someone named to the OU faculty or staff. I stressed that this would not be good for the university, an institution in which, as an alumnus, he must take considerable pride. After listening for several minutes, he finally broke in: "I see what you mean. I won't press for this appointment, but I don't ever want to hear of your hiring anyone suggested by any other member of the legislature." I assured him that I would hold the line, though suggestions from any source would be considered strictly on their merits.

The legislator must have spread the word around the statehouse, because for the next twenty-five years I received no pressure from anyone to make a staff or faculty appointment. I do not mean to imply that the university was completely free of political influence in making appointments. I am sure that our local senator, who was a staunch supporter of the University, was occasionally able to persuade OU's superintendent of buildings and grounds to employ maintenance workers.

Now and then I received a letter from a legislator or the governor strongly recommending someone for a position, but in nearly every such instance the letter was followed by a phone call or accompanied by a note on a separate sheet of paper telling me that the letter had been written at the request of the individual, that the individual had been given a copy of the letter of recommendation, but that I was to use my own good judgment in the situation. One governor sent me perhaps a dozen such letters, with the same handwritten but unsigned accompanying note.

Shortly before I became president of OU, the Oklahoma State System of Higher Education was established by an amendment to the State constitution that was approved by the people of Oklahoma in a special election on March 11, 1941. The amendment also provided for a coordinating board of control, to be known as the Oklahoma State Regents for Higher Education with a chancellor as chief executive officer. Instead of dealing directly with the legislature in making requests for appropriations, the schools included in the system made their requests through the state board. This provided some insulation from political influence, though when the budget for higher education was presented to the legislature, it was necessary for the president of each institution to appear before the combined appropriations committees of the house and senate to defend or interpret the requests included for his institution.

On one occasion in the mid-1950s I had an interesting experience with the system. I was given thirty minutes before the committees to explain the University's fiscal needs for the following biennium. During the presentation I felt very confident; I was sure that I was being articulate and persuasive—even convincing. After I had finished and left the lectern, feeling rather smug and self-satisfied, the chairman of the combined committees invited questions. A corpulent senator, who had been seated on the front row directly before me as I spoke, said, "I'd like to ask the good doctor why he thinks he needs so much money to run the University of Oklahoma." Completely deflated, and realizing that I had probably made no impression on the rest of the committee members, I thought of the Big Red football team that Bud Wilkinson had coached to a national championship and the statewide enthusiasm it had engendered. I replied to the senator's question, "Well, I'd like to try to build a university the football team can be proud of." The wry comment brought a burst of laughter—and may well have produced better support of the budget request than the talk I had given so confidently.

That remark attracted wider attention than anything else I said during my presidency. It appeared in many of the nation's larger newspapers and at least one foreign one. *Time* and *Life* magazines picked it up, and one day I received a note from *Readers' Digest,* along with a small check, saying that the magazine wanted to print the comment with my permission. Several years later they used the same item again, but there was no additional check. I didn't complain, however, reflecting that it was the only printed material of any kind for which I had received any payment.

It was inevitable, of course, that I should have other adventures with the legislature. For many years it had been the custom to provide two tickets to the football games to each member of the legislature and other important public officials. The tickets were intended for the personal use of the recipients; they were not to be given to others. To ensure this, the legislators were to pick up their tickets on the day of the game. One fall in the 1950s, while the OU football team was in the process of winning forty-seven consecutive games—a record that still stands—a member of the state senate came to my office and asked me to have his tickets mailed to him a few days before the games; the senator was a medical doctor, and he often saw patients on game days. He found it very difficult to get to the campus in time to pick up his tickets.

I explained that I could not deviate from a policy that had been set by the University regents. Obviously disgruntled, he left with the comment that he was receiving much better treatment from other state institutions and that he would keep this incident in mind.

During the next legislative session, when the university's budget was being considered, the senator decided that he would investigate the University's expenditures of the past biennium. When I learned of this, I suspected that his sleuthing was related to the ticket incident. In any event, he discovered, probably to his satisfaction, that the University had spent appropriated funds on items that he thought were not needed. Included on his list were an air-conditioner for the guest room of the president's house, an oil portrait of the president costing $1,200, two Aeronica airplanes for

35

flight training (surplus planes were available from the federal government), and, most important of all, a set of earrings and a brazier from an Egyptian tomb.

When the budget request for higher education was presented a few days later, the senator asked for the floor and announced that he wanted to make some comments about the University's expenditures of money appropriated in the past. He read a long list of doubtful items, including the air-conditioner, the portrait of the president, and the airplanes, and he wound up with the startling announcement that OU had spent a substantial amount of money on earrings and "brassieres."

Headlines in the *Oklahoma City Times* that afternoon announced the startling revelation, and the accompanying story reported that a senate committee had been appointed to get an explanation from the University and report back to the senate. A few days later I was summoned to appear before the committee.

I took with me Roscoe Cate, financial vice-president of the university, who knew far more about university expenditures than I did. While we were waiting in the outer office of the chairman of the investigating committee, several reporters, led by Bill Henthorne of the *Tulsa World*, approached us. Henthorne asked: "What are you fellows going to tell the committee? Are you going to break down and confess that you have wasted state money or are you going to insist that your expenditures were necessary to develop a great football team?" Cate, after a moment's hesitation, replied, "With the exception of the brassieres, we're going to make a clean breast of the whole thing." The delighted Henthorne turned to me and asked, "Can I print that?"

I replied: "I surely hope you won't. I wouldn't like for the senate to get the impression that we are approaching this investigation in a spirit of levity. It's grim business with us." Neither Henthorne nor the other reporters included Cate's remark in their stories.

Our session with the senate committee was not at all unpleasant. Asked about the air-conditioner in the president's home, I explained that it was for the comfort of distinguished visitors who came to the state during the summer months. Sir Alexander Fleming, the discoverer of penicillin, was such a visitor. After my explanation a member of the committee said that he could see why the air-conditioner had been bought. It was important to make a good impression on visitors to the University and the state. He saw no objection to air-conditioning the guest room, he said, adding, with great sincerity, "as long as the president and his wife don't sleep there."

In replying to the question about the airplanes, I explained that surplus planes available from the armed forces were far too sophisticated for teaching beginning flying and far too expensive to operate. Members of the committee nodded their heads in understanding.

Then a member of the committee said, "You'll have to admit that having a portrait of the president of the university painted at a cost of $1,200 was an unneeded extravagance." I quickly agreed, saying that I had not been in favor of having the portrait painted because it was intended to hang with portraits of past presidents of the University. The regents had ordered it painted. I thought it too early in my administration to think about being a past president. In fact, it had made me a little nervous. I then added, as ingenuously as possible, that, of course, only one portrait was painted of each president and that if the regents did not change presidents too often the cost would not be burdensome—the $1,200 could be amortized over a number of years. Several members of the committee nodded in sympathetic agreement.

37

There was no problem about the earrings and the brazier. While some members of the committee may have thought that antique earrings and brazier might be of doubtful usefulness for instructional purposes, they were more amused by the senator's confusion of "brazier" and "brassiere" than concerned about the cost of the two items.

When the committee reported back to the senate later in the week, it gave the University a clean bill of health in expenditures, and salty Jim Nance, the senator from Purcell, commented, "It would appear that someone has been making mountains out of molehills." The newspapers apparently agreed with Nance.

There were, of course, some grim times with the legislature. During the early 1950s the legislature investigated the University for evidence of the presence of Communists and, though it found little or no evidence, enacted legislation requiring state employees to sign a ridiculous loyalty oath, one provision of which required the signer to bear arms in defense of the country, thus, among other things, depriving the University of the services of visiting professors from other countries. Fortunately, the United States Supreme Court declared the oath law unconstitutional a few months later.

I see no need for you to be apprehensive about dealing with your state legislature. You will find it a sound practice, however, to treat all legislators—and other political figures—with firm respect. You should give a little extra attention to your local delegation, but be sure to do so impartially. I think that legislatures have improved in quality through the years. This is certainly true in Oklahoma's state capitol, where I have noted increasing respect and concern for education at all levels.

A friendly press can help you immeasurably in dealing with your legislature. I found it best to be completely frank with reporters and other members of the fourth estate. I never tried to conceal anything, because I knew that they would ferret out the truth and resent my making them do extra work, or, if they did not find the truth, write stories more unfavorable to the University than the truth. I never tried to give information off the record. Reporters don't like this approach. On some occasions I would comment that if certain things that I told them were used in their stories I would be embarrassed. During the nearly twenty-five years that I was in office, I do not recall any reporter using material that I had said would be embarrassing to me.

The point of all of this is that, at a time when you may be having some problems with legislators or other political figures, a friendly press will surely present your University's position fairly.

All good wishes to you and your fine family.

Affectionately,

On Public Speaking

Dear Bill,

So you are reasonably pleased with the way things are going in your new job but are somewhat dismayed by the number of requests you have received to speak before diverse groups. That is not surprising, and I can understand your concern that the time involved in meeting these many requests could better be spent studying the immediate problems of your institution and planning for their solution. I assure you, however, that every newly appointed president of a college or university has been confronted with the same problem.

The situation is perhaps worse in a public university, because the people of the state feel that they own the institution and want to find out what the new person at the helm is like. You will be asked to appear before most of the civic clubs and chambers of commerce in the state, especially those in the larger metropolitan areas. Then there will be church groups and various clubs and other organizations. A presidential colleague of mine once said that a new university president will likely make as many speeches "as Samson slew Philistines" and added, "In many cases he will use the same implement." You will, of course, try to avoid the latter.

I remember well my own difficulties during my first year as president of OU. I was especially handicapped by the fact that, as a scientist, I had disciplined myself not to talk unless I knew what I was talking about. Too, it had been necessary for me to develop brevity in speaking and writing—never to use two words when one would suffice. Suddenly I was thrust into a situation where I was invited to speak on a great variety of subjects, whether or not I knew anything about them and, taking cue from the many speakers I had heard, never to use one word when three or four could be worked in.

However, I was fairly successful in avoiding unfamiliar subjects; no matter what I was asked to talk about, I spoke on something relating to the University. In explaining my insistence on choosing my own topic, I used a story that I believe should be credited to Irvin S. Cobb. It involved a professor of history who was greatly interested in the life and affairs of Patrick Henry. So great was the professor's obsession with that distinguished critic of the Stamp Act that, when giving a speech, regardless of the topic assigned to him, he ended up talking about Patrick Henry.

The professor belonged to a Rotary Club, and one day his fellow Rotarians plotted to create a situation in which it would be impossible for him to mention Patrick Henry. For one of their programs they planned a series of extemporaneous speeches to be given by members of their club, and the professor of history was invited, with three others, to participate. The plot included the provision that the topic or subject for each speaker would not be announced until he was on his feet ready to begin delivery. The history professor was scheduled to speak last in the series of talks. When his time came, he rose to his feet, and the toastmaster promptly gave him the subject "horse colic." The professor looked nonplused for a moment. Then his face brightened, and he said: "My fellow Rotarians, before we get down to the business of exploring this subject in depth and detail, let us first generalize concerning the nature of horse colic. Gentlemen, horse colic is nothing more nor less than a substantial bubble of air wandering hither and yon within the internal confines of a horse, shouting, 'Give me liberty or give me death!'"

Following this story, which usually received a favorable response, I would explain that, although I had been invited to speak on another topic, there were some things about the University of Oklahoma that I thought they should know.

Sometimes, when the situation seemed to call for a little additional humor, I would follow with another anecdote concerning speech titles that was passed on to me by Savoie Lottinville, the distinguished director emeritus of the University of Oklahoma Press.

Lottinville's story was about a psychology professor who had given a speech one afternoon to a women's club. His subject had been "Sex on the University Campus." When the professor went home that evening, his wife asked him what his day had been like, and he told her that he had given a speech to a women's club. She then asked him what his subject had been. Perhaps not wishing to get involved in additional discussion of the subject on which he had spent so much time that afternoon, he told her that he had talked on "sailing." She looked at him a little doubtfully but let the matter drop.

Two or three days later his wife met a woman who had heard the talk. The woman said to her, "My, your husband certainly gave our club a splendid talk the other day." The wife replied, "Well, I don't see how he could have. He doesn't know anything about the subject. He's only tried it twice. The first time the wind blew his hat off, and the second time he got sick to his stomach."

It is interesting to reflect that Lottinville's anecdote could not have been safely told before a mixed audience in my day.

Humor at the beginning of a talk and intermittently

later, can be of great help in gaining and holding an audience's attention, but it must always relate in some way to the subject under discussion. Unrelated stories are likely to fall flat, especially with sophisticated audiences.

Early in my career I learned not to talk too long on any occasion. In those days, civic clubs expected a speaker to talk for no more than about twenty minutes. I've noticed that in recent years the time has been shortened to twelve or fifteen minutes. On many occasions when I spoke to civic clubs I promised to try not to speak beyond twenty minutes and then tell an anecdote that had appeared in a magazine (I've forgotten which one) following President Harry Truman's upset victory in the presidential race back in 1948, after the Gallup Poll had indicated that Thomas E. Dewey would win by a substantial margin. As near as I can recall, the story went as follows:

There was a young man in a community who did a great deal of public speaking. As time went on, he became noted for his ability to time his speeches to exactly twenty minutes. Those with the responsibility of arranging after-dinner programs came to rely on his skillful timing and were able to structure their programs effectively.

All went well until one day when the speaker appeared before a civic group. He spoke twenty minutes and didn't stop. Those in attendance, especially the toastmaster, listened with surprise as he spoke for a second twenty-minute period—then with consternation as he went on through a third before finally coming to a stop.

Afterward the toastmaster said to him, "What in the world happened to you? You have a reputation of being able to speak exactly twenty minutes and we were depending on that today, but instead you spoke an hour."

The speaker replied, "I'm sorry about that, but to be very truthful I must admit that some time ago I learned that if I placed a cough drop of a certain brand under my tongue I could speak for exactly twenty minutes by which time it would be completely dissolved. Since then it has been my custom before starting to slip a cough drop under my tongue and keep speaking as long as I feel it there. Today I spoke for an hour before I discovered that I didn't have a cough drop under my tongue at all—I had an old 'Dewey for President' button."

You asked whether I have any rule of thumb for deciding which speaking invitations to accept. I can say only that I think that during your first year you should accept practically every invitation you receive, though you should ration your time by deciding how many you will give each week. You may soon find yourself fully scheduled for months in advance, but you cannot safely refuse any invitation. After a year or so the requests will diminish somewhat, and as time goes on, you can carefully become a bit more selective in your acceptances.

There are several ways in which you can conserve your speechmaking activities. For instance, the city of Norman and nearby Oklahoma City have many civic clubs. In Norman I was invited to speak before each of the civic clubs and the Chamber of Commerce every year. I finally persuaded the local clubs and the chamber to have a joint meeting each fall in the ballroom of the Student Union Building, at which I made a report on the state of the university. I worked out a similar plan for Oklahoma City. That saved a great deal of time, and you may find the idea useful.

Good luck with your speechmaking. I don't think you'll have too much difficulty. Don't try to compose a separate speech for every occasion. Develop "core" talks that can be modified for the various occasions.

Affectionately,

More on Faculty Relations

October 15

Dear Bill,

I am glad you reminded me to send you some comments about the talk you will make at your general faculty meeting this fall. After your governing board, the most sensitive group of people you will deal with is the faculty. I have already stressed the importance of the faculty as the basic constituent of any university, and I have stressed the responsibility of the president to provide a favorable ambience for faculty effort—including efficient physical facilities, adequate salaries, and reasonable financing of creative activities, as well as mediation, coordination, and initiation when such may be desirable or necessary.

But the president has a responsibility to the faculty much more basic than any of the above. He is responsible for the quality of the faculty—its origin and maintenance. It is up to him to see that high quality is maintained and improved as time goes on, through the careful selection of new personnel.

Of course, you will not be directly responsible for the selection of new faculty members for your institution. Times have changed markedly since my alma mater, the University of Chicago, got under way back in 1891. That institution's first president, William Rainey Harper, bolstered by millions of dollars supplied by John D. Rockefeller, personally recruited his institution's entire first faculty. Able to offer annual salaries of $7,000 for full professors, while the nation's average was perhaps $2,000, Harper was able to pick and choose with great discrimination. He mercilessly raided the faculties of the country's institutions—in some instances

45

taking entire departments. He even persuaded nine college or university presidents to accept professorial status at his fledgling institution. One of the presidents, John Merle Coulter, was for many years head of the department in which I did my doctoral work.

Harper's spectacular success in recruiting Chicago's first faculty greatly impressed at least one of those who followed him in the presidency. When Robert Maynard Hutchins, boy prodigy from the Yale Law School, was installed as fifth president of the university in 1929, at the age of thirty, he said in his inaugural address, "Had the first Chicago faculty met in a tent, this would still have been a great university." Certainly irrelevant, but perhaps of some interest to you, is the fact that I received my doctorate at the end of the fall quarter of 1929, at the first commencement ceremony over which Hutchins presided. As I walked up to be hooded in the beautiful new university chapel, I thought that Hutchins looked more like a choirboy than a university president.

While, as I have said, university presidents no longer participate directly in the selection of faculty members, they still play an important role in the process. Recommendations for new faculty members which usually originate in departmental selection committees, come to the president for approval by way of the office of the dean of the college and the university provost. In many universities only the dean of the undergraduate college is involved in the selection process. At the University of Oklahoma, where there are three strata of colleges involved with each appointment—the University College, the specific undergraduate college, and the Graduate College—I found it advisable many years ago to get the opinions of all three deans. I did so because I thought that a dean could not be expected to be responsible for the development of his college unless he had a voice in the selection of faculty personnel.

Of course, the president will not have time to explore carefully the credentials of all the candidates who are recommended; that responsibility should be turned over to the deans and the provost. But he can meet his responsibility for ensuring a quality faculty by using great care at the time a departmental chairman, a dean, or a provost is named. He should make sure that each person appointed to an academic administrative post understands what a high-quality university is all about—good teaching, research, and public service. Having done this, he will need to rely, except in rare instances, on the recommendations of the departments, deans, and provost for additions to the faculty.

While this method of recruitment works well in most cases, occasionally difficulties may develop. It is inevitable that each department should seek its own personnel without help from deans, provosts, or presidents. In some institutions the departmental chairman has the responsibility; in others a committee may be involved. Whether a chairman or a committee makes the search, there is always a possibility that the best possible candidates available will not be recommended for appointment. The chairman or members of the selections committee, through feelings of insecurity, may be reluctant to recommend superior candidates who may soon achieve greater prestige than their own.

I suspected this to be the case in several departments at the University of Oklahoma—especially in the Fine Arts Departments. In some instances it almost seemed that a conspiracy existed to preserve a comfortably mediocre departmental program. I finally decided, however, that such an attitude could develop in any department with a preponderance of older teachers who had anchored peacefully in their academic harbors and were unwilling to set sail again. A highly competent, energetic younger person could cause such a group no end of embarrassment.

Such situations are very difficult for a president to deal with. On two or three occasions at OU the problem was solved by bringing in a very able departmental chairman and giving him more than the usual authority in departmental affairs with complete responsibility for recruitment. Only once did this method fail, and it failed because the new chairman used a meat-ax approach to departmental problems when a carefully used scalpel would have been much more effective.

Sometimes deans, especially deans of professional schools, are afflicted with insecurity. For several years I watched the progress of a professional school at OU flounder because the dean refused to approve the hiring of any faculty member who might challenge his prestige. He was not content merely to stand head and shoulders above his faculty but wanted to stand waist-high. After I became president, I tried to persuade him to change his ways. He responded with a letter to the chairman of the Board of Regents charging me with meddling in the internal affairs of his college and being dishonest in dealing with him. He asked for a complete investigation by the regents and hinted that my removal from office might be the best solution. At its next meeting the governing board removed him from office, appointed a three-man committee to look after the college, and instructed me to find a new dean. I hope you don't have problems of this kind; if you do, I know that you will find a way to solve them.

But your immediate concern is not the selection of new faculty but how to get along well with those you have inherited from your predecessor. In this connection I might mention the problem that is causing concern on a great many university campuses, and certainly at the University of Oklahoma—the criteria to be used in granting promotions, salary increases, and tenure. There are several facets to the problem, but the one I hear discussed most frequently at OU is the "publish or perish" edict, in vogue at many institutions, but proposed and partly implemented here only during the past decade by a provost who is no longer with us.

Immediately after World War II, when enrollment in the nation's colleges and universities soared from a prewar total of one million to more than seven million in less than a decade, I gave much thought to what could be expected from collegiate faculties. While I knew that a university could not be great, or even very good, without an outstanding program of research and publication, it did not seem reasonable to expect this kind of creative activity from everyone. Some, perhaps many, faculty members might find fulfillment through excellent teaching and public service.

I have always been convinced that research and publication should be attempted only by those who are genuinely interested in some problem—never because of a requirement by an institution. I have been equally convinced that there are not enough individuals in the academic world with genuine research talent to staff the country's universities. To require publication from all would mean diverting faculty attention from teaching and result in the production of printed matter much of which was not worth the space it would occupy on a library shelf.

For these reasons until very recently criteria for advancement at OU were demonstrated excellence in two of three areas of university activity—teaching, research, and public service. I still believe they were sound criteria.

With respect to your approaching speech before the general faculty, I suggest that you not be too specific in making commitments. While you doubtless have plans and objectives for your institution, it might be best to mention them only in the context that you expect to take them up with your faculty senate. The theme of your talk might well be that you hope to make a very good institution better but that the thoughts of all members of the faculty will be necessary to accomplish this effectively. You will say this not merely to placate the faculty but because it is true. With the cooperation of your faculty there is virtually no end to what you can accomplish—especially if you don't care who gets the credit.

You may want to include in your remarks an acknowledgement that the faculty is really the university and that the administration exists to hold things together and create a favorable environment on the campus so that the faculty can get things done. William S. Banowsky, who became the tenth president of the University of Oklahoma in the late summer of 1978, handled all of this very well when he first spoke to the faculty. He said that the faculty and the library were the basic ingredients of the university and then followed with the disarming oversimplification that the administration was really a service division, chiefly responsible for such matters as replacing light bulbs.

While rummaging through my files the other day, in preparation for finally yielding the office space that I have occupied in the Botany and Microbiology Building since I retired, I came across a copy of the first speech that I gave to the faculty after I was named acting president of the University of Oklahoma back in 1943. It occurred to me that you might be interested in seeing it, and a copy is enclosed [see Appendix 1]. While it will not be much, if any, use to you as you prepare your remarks, it does deal with problems that have always existed on college and university campuses—problems that will never be completely solved but, through being illuminated occasionally, may be kept from growing worse. Perhaps you will find an idea or two in it.

Affectionately,

On Student Relations

October 28

Dear Bill,

I am glad that you found the copy of my speech helpful. As I continue to cull my files, I'll be on the alert for other talks that might be useful to you. I suspect that, generally speaking, the same kind of talks have been given by state university presidents throughout the land—and throughout time. Three presidents have served the University of Oklahoma since I retired in 1968, and while reading newspaper reports of their talks, I have been increasingly surprised by how similar their remarks were to my own of so many years before. For the most part, the speeches covered university promotion and interpretation. Institutional problems —usually involving finances—and their proposed solutions seem to change little as time passes.

I am pleased also that you are giving serious thought to your relations with students (I avoid using the term "student body"; to me it classifies the campus as a morgue). Although some members of the faculty may occasionally be inclined to regard them as necessary nuisances, students are the reason for a university's existence. It is important for you to be on good terms with students, though you may not have time to know many of them personally.

Like you, I realized early in my presidency at OU the need for frequent contacts with at least representative groups of students. In the beginning I left such contacts largely to chance. I merely accepted invitations to speak at meetings of campus organizations, and I established an open-door policy whereby students could come to my office without appointments. I set aside one hour each afternoon for the latter

51

visitations, but I would see any student who came to my office when I did not have another appointment.

I soon found that this arrangement did not work out too well. The only organization that seemed interested in hearing me talk was the Panhellenic Council. Of course, we were just a bit beyond midway through World War II, and many student organizations had been inactivated for the duration of the war. Students did not come to my office in great numbers. Some of them probably thought that my time was too valuable to be spent with individual students, and others may have stayed away because of shyness. After the war the situation changed markedly when great numbers of veterans descended on the campus. Groups of them came to see me quite frequently about a great variety of matters— methods of teaching, prerequisites for courses, accelerated programs, and the lack of student housing, among others. But these groups did not take advantage of the open-door policy; almost invariably they made appointments with my secretary.

One of my predecessors at OU, William Bennett Bizzell, who retired in 1941, had a "President's Class" composed of thirty-five or forty carefully selected students in their third year at the University. He met with the group weekly in the president's house, and they discussed various subjects related to the humanities. When I became president, I considered the possibility of reactivating the President's Class, but David Burr, one of my young administrative associates, countered with the suggestion that it might be a good idea for me to get acquainted with at least a core of the best students who entered the university each fall. With his help we organized the "President's Leadership Class," consisting of about sixty freshmen chosen by a committee.

Each summer an invitation to apply for admission to the class was sent to outstanding high-school seniors who would enter the university that fall. That usually produced about two hundred applicants, from whom the class members were selected. The class met monthly during the school year and enjoyed several privileges—including special instruction on how to use the library and the opportunity to hear talks by the best of the OU faculty. The program was very successful, and all my successors to the presidency saw fit to continue it. Members of the class told me that they profited greatly from the experience, and I profited in later years, when some of them were elected to public office or gained other important positions.

When this program was in the planning stage, I remember thinking how helpful it would be if a university president could look into the future and know which of his students would become members of the legislature, governors, members of Congress, or heads of corporations. But, as prescience was never one of my strong points, and as years of watching election results passed, I gradually realized that there was practically no way anyone could be ruled out. That, I suppose, is one of the basic strengths of our country.

The only other arrangement I made to see a student group on a regular schedule came during the 1960s—the decade of student confrontations. I was initially warned of impending campus unrest when Clark Kerr, president of the University of California, generally conceded to be one of the leading academic administrators in the nation, lost his job as a result of student rebellion. When the turbulent movement, which started on the two coasts, reached the midlands—the Universities of Wisconsin, Michigan, and finally Kansas—I decided that defensive maneuvers were indicated for the University of Oklahoma. I invited each of several major student organizations on the campus to elect a representative for membership on a student council, or committee, that I was organizing. I have forgotten how many organizations were included, but I do recall that there were representatives from the Student Senate, the Interfraternity Council, the Panhellenic Council, the Independent Student Association, and the commuting students.

I met with the committee each Saturday morning at nine o'clock, and by eleven I had a pretty good idea of what the student population thought was wrong on the campus. In addition, however, I had had a chance to interpret, as best I could, the university's side of the problems to the students. These sessions had two major advantages: they gave me an opportunity during the following week to take any necessary corrective action, and they gave the members of the student committee time to report back to their organizations and explain, if necessary, why the administration had been unable to solve a particular problem. I am convinced that these weekly sessions were the major factor in keeping the University of Oklahoma free of student confrontations until 1968, when I retired from the presidency.

Only one serious student crisis threatened to develop during my administration. It centered on a housing problem. As a result of enrollment projections made by the Oklahoma State Regents for Higher Education, the University regents issued bonds and constructed housing to take care of what it considered the university's share of the predicted increase. By the time the new housing was finished and ready for occupancy, the state regents had decided that the junior-college movement in the state should be encouraged, and several new colleges were launched, including the excellent Oscar Rose Junior College in Midwest City, a few miles northeast of Norman. Loss of freshmen and sophomore enrollment to the junior colleges put university housing in a temporarily overbuilt situation.

The contracts with the bond buyers provided that the

University regents would require student occupancy of the housing sufficient to generate an income of 130 percent of what was needed to retire the bonds on schedule and pay the interest on those still outstanding. Failure to meet the conditions of the contract with the bond buyers meant that the regents would be personally responsible for the housing indebtedness. During past years the University's housing indebtedness had been handled easily by requiring freshmen and sophomores to live in the housing but making it optional for juniors and seniors to live there. However, with the completion of the twelve-story complex later named Couch Center, it became necessary to require all single students (with certain exceptions, such as commuters and those whose homes were in Norman) to occupy university housing. It would be an understatement to say that the announcement of the requirement caused a sensation on campus. A student rebellion seemed imminent.

After hearing many rumors of angry student reaction, I decided that a protest meeting with the students would be necessary to clear the air. Such a meeting would give the protesters an opportunity to tell me in no uncertain terms how they felt about the new ruling and give me an opportunity to explain that the regents were really helpless in the situation: their only alternative was to assume personal responsibility for the University's housing debt—actually a financial impossibility, because at that time the combined resources of the board probably would have fallen far short of the several million dollars the university owed.

In addition to giving me an opportunity to explain the regents' dilemma to the students, I thought that a confrontation would provide an opportunity to tell the students about a new plan for "adult living" in university housing that had been hastily developed in my office as soon as we saw that a crisis might be developing.

Until that time the mores of a large portion of the mid-continent had dictated that colleges and universities act in loco parentis for their students. There were many rules to be obeyed—including no visitation in rooms by members of the opposite sex, no possession of alcoholic beverages, and a score of others, which students of today would think preposterous. It seemed to be a good time to experiment with a plan whereby most rules of this nature would be abolished and the students required only to live by the laws of the land. This, we decided, might be tried on a limited basis in certain sections of the housing for single students occupied by juniors and seniors. We suspected that the public would not accept an immediate wholesale abandonment of regulations but might tolerate an experimental approach on a small scale. If the plan seemed to work, it could be extended to all housing for juniors and seniors.

The next step was to arrange a student confrontation. At this point I received the enthusiastic participation of the student committee with which I had been meeting each Saturday morning. The committee took the lead in calling a student protest meeting for 4:30 on a Friday afternoon. I suggested Friday because I figured that students would be thinking about their weekend activities, and I suggested 4:30 because an hour or so later they would also be thinking about dinner—not being stuck at the back of the cafeteria lines and that sort of thing.

The meeting went very well. We spent the first hour listening to a series of student speakers who denounced the new housing requirement and, incidentally, many other shortcomings of the administration and regents. The many denunciations, some couched in picturesque terms, seemed to have a therapeutic effect on the several hundred who had assembled west of the Union Building. Then, at what I considered the proper time, I made my own remarks. I explained very carefully the problem the regents faced, and I described our experimental plan for adult living. Then I asked for questions and further comments from the students. During the question-and-answer period, the students began drifting away, beginning about 5:45, just as I had expected them to.

Finally only a handful was left, and as I looked around, it seemed that the news reporters, in abundance at the beginning of the meeting, had departed also. At this point a young man said to me: "Now let me get this plan for adult living straight. Suppose it is eleven o'clock at night, and I am in my room with my girl and a bottle of bourbon. What ———?" Knowing that he was going to ask me whether this would be all right with the university, and not wanting to be put on the spot in such fashion, I broke in with the comment, "Well, that surely is a happy thought, isn't it?" But while I evaded the embarrassment of giving the boy an answer, I created some embarrassment for myself through the fact that one of the local papers carried a report of our exchange the next day. One lone reporter, whom I had not recognized, had not left the meeting.

I hope that the above perhaps too numerous paragraphs will give you an idea or two. I hope also that you will find dealing with your students as pleasant and rewarding as I found it to be at OU. I really did enjoy them; in retrospect I even enjoyed the happy little group that used to come by the president's house each Saturday evening after a student hangout down the street had closed at midnight, shouting, "Hi, George! How're ya doin', ol' boy, ol' boy?"

Affectionately,

More on Student Relations

Dear Bill,

Thanks for your prompt response to my last letter. Obviously you're enjoying your contacts with students—except possibly the occasional nuisance phone calls you have received. The latter can become a real problem, as I discovered within a few weeks after moving into the president's house at OU. Fun-loving students, and perhaps a few nonstudents, thought it great sport to call late at night and make false reports on what was happening about the campus. At the time my home phone was connected with the University switchboard and, of course, listed in the campus directory. Cleo and I occasionally discussed the possibility of having a private line installed with an unlisted number. We were reluctant to do this, because there were certain advantages to being on the switchboard. But a telephone adventure with a student late one Saturday night (really Sunday morning) convinced us that something had to be done.

Cleo and I got home about 11:45 that night after attending a university function of some kind. I was tired—exhausted, actually—and I went to bed immediately. Cleo proceeded more leisurely with the nightly ritual of attention to hair and face. I had just dozed off when I was awakened by the telephone.

Cleo answered the call. Checking with her later, I learned that the conversation developed somewhat as follows. The caller said, "I'm a student at the university and I have a problem I'd like to discuss with President Cross."

Cleo responded, "My husband is asleep. Why don't you

just describe the problem to me, and I'll decide whether it's necessary to awaken him."

"Well, it's like this. My fraternity had a dinner in the Union Building tonight, and shortly after eating, I became ill. I went to the men's room to relieve myself, and while I was throwing up, I lost a new partial denture in the toilet bowl. I was so sick that I flushed the bowl before I realized what was happening. It was a two-tooth partial which I got just this week, and I paid eighty-five dollars for it. I would like for a university plumber to go to the Union Building and try to find it for me."

"I don't think that any university plumber would be interested in going to the Union at this time of night to look for your denture."

"I know that a plumber wouldn't be interested in looking for *my* denture, but I thought if President Cross would tell him that he had lost *his* denture, he could be persuaded to go."

Cleo assured the young man that this was not a satisfactory solution to his problem but that likely there would be no activity in the men's room on Sunday and that I would have a plumber explore the situation early Monday morning. Although obviously disappointed, the boy agreed, and the conversation ended. Sure enough, we sent a plumber to the men's room in the Union Building early Monday morning, and, after considerable effort, he found the missing denture, which was returned to the boy. The boy is now a businessman in Norman. A few years ago Cleo made a speech to the local historical society in which she told the story. After the meeting a man in the audience identified himself as the one who had made the midnight call.

Reflecting on the incident the next week, Cleo and I decided that we could solve future problems of this kind by instructing the operator of the university switchboard not to put any calls through to us after 10:00 P.M. In event of emergency the operator was to refer the call to the super-intendent of buildings and grounds, who would decide whether to put it through to us.

This arrangement protected our hours of sleep pretty well. As a matter of fact, it gave us rather good protection against nuisance calls of all kinds because people are likely to select late hours for such pranks.

Of course, there were many attempts to reach us on what were claimed to be emergencies, but such calls were success-fully screened out over a period of more than twenty years — except on one occasion.

One night in December, 1958, the phone rang at 11:30. Apprehensively I picked up the receiver and heard the university operator say that Bud Wilkinson, then at the height of his career as football coach at OU, had been seriously injured in an automobile accident near Ada, Oklahoma, and that someone in Ada wanted to give me the details. Chilled by the news, I said that I would accept the call. Moments later I was in conversation with someone who was obviously at a party situation, to judge by the noise and laughter in the background. My caller hastened to assure me that Bud Wilkinson had not been in an automobile accident, as far as he knew, but that he wanted to discuss with me Wilkinson's decision not to permit his best quarterback to play in the Orange Bowl game that was coming up in a couple of weeks.

I was familiar with the situation. Wilkinson had dropped the boy from the squad when he learned that he had not been attending classes. The boy would have been eligible to play, because he was in good academic standing when the fall semester opened. But Wilkinson thought that to take advan-tage of this technicality would be unethical, and he ruled on that basis. My caller took the position that it was ridiculous not to take advantage of the technical eligibility of the quarterback—that I should overrule the coach and insist that the boy be allowed to rejoin the squad. He stated, with emphasis, that there was no possibility of winning the bowl game without the great quarterback's help and that I alone would be responsible for the team's loss if I didn't follow his suggestion. At this point I placed the receiver back on the phone and returned to bed. Later developments showed that my caller had exaggerated the importance of the delinquent quarterback in OU football. Wilkinson worked constantly with his second-string quarterback in preparing for the trip to Miami, and OU defeated Syracuse University 21 to 6 on January 1, 1959.

Incidentally, you might be interested in a story related to that game that I didn't tell in *Presidents Can't Punt.* Prentice Gautt, the first black athlete to play football at the University of Oklahoma, was easily the star of the game. As fullback, he ran wild against Syracuse—through the line and on sweeps—and as a linebacker (players were used on both offense and defense in those days) he performed brilliantly. Glowing accolades of his performance appeared in the papers the next morning, and it was the consensus of sportswriters that he had easily been the best player on the field.

That morning several individuals were lounging in the lobby of the Miami hotel where the OU players and fans were staying. Several of them were reading newspapers, doubtless Jack Bell's account of the game in the *Miami Herald,* when Gautt came strolling through accompanied by two or three teammates. About midway in the lobby an obese man arose from his chair and planted himself, a bit unsteadily, in front of Gautt. The man said in a loud voice, "You black son-of-a-bitch!" There was an immediate, ominous silence in the lobby, as those who had heard waited for what would happen next. Gautt's face turned grim, and his body stiffened. But he restrained himself, possibly because he realized that the fellow had been drinking, and during the pause the man put his arm around Gautt's shoulder and announced, "You black son-of-a-bitch, you're the best God-damned football player that I ever saw on a football field!" Several Oklahomans and others relaxed somewhat in hopeful relief, but it was obvious that the incident had not yet ended. Gautt was still tense. Gradually, however, the grim look on his face and his perceptibly quivering body quieted. He ended the dramatic moment, saying, "Thank you, sir," and went on his way, leaving a rather limp audience behind. It is difficult for me to recall a more suspenseful incident.

But I'm afraid I have drifted from the subject of what to do about nuisance phone calls—became a victim of the elderlys' inclination to reminisce. I'll sum it all up by saying that, in my opinion, there is no way that a university president can have a listed number in a telephone directory. An unlisted number should pose no problems; his administrative colleagues will surely reach him in times of need.

Affectionately,

On Student Demonstrations

November 15

Dear Bill,

Your account of the group of boisterous students who assembled in your front yard protesting new parking regulations and other campus matters brought nostalgic memories of student-group action at OU. But it also gave me the impression that you may have tended to overreact a bit to the incident. This type of thing is commonplace on university campuses.

As you surely must recall from your own undergraduate years, students are amazingly innovative in coming up with outlandish ideas during their spare time. If I remember correctly, the goldfish-swallowing craze had just passed out of vogue at the time you were beginning your freshman year. Then came an impressive effort to set records of how many could crowd into a telephone booth and, later, into a Volkswagen. You will recall the panty raids of midcentury and the more recent "streaking," which was viewed with disfavor by many of the older folk. You can expect practically anything to happen on a university campus and with it, of course, embarrassment for the president.

I have always been interested in how student group action gets under way. Usually, I think, the idea originates in the minds of a few who sell the idea to others in various ways. I recall one successful demonstration of this sales approach that occurred at OU many years ago. It had rained the first four days of Homecoming Week, and the students were unable to work on house decorations and floats for the homecoming parade. But the skies cleared on Thursday afternoon, and a very small group of students decided that Friday classes should be canceled so that they could complete their preparations for homecoming on time. This small group went about the housing area shouting, "No school tomorrow! Meet at Campus Corner at five o'clock!" Attracted by this prospect, dozens of students assembled at Campus Corner and then marched about the campus shouting in unison, "No school tomorrow!" The noise aroused the curiosity of about two thousand individuals—students and nonstudents—who when they considered the group was large enough, marched to the president's house to give the head man their message. Learning that I was out of town, they went to a vice-president's home, where a compromise was arranged, giving the students Friday afternoon off to complete their homecoming floats.

While that might be considered almost standard procedure in getting such activities under way, the last major event of its kind during my administration developed in a somewhat more complicated manner.

In early October, 1967, the members of the OU Chapter of Students for a Democratic Society (you will remember that somewhat radical national organization, which had chapters on many university campuses) carefully planned what they announced would be "Gentle Thursday." They would spend the day, they said, lounging on campus lawns, reading poetry, chatting, and otherwise participating in "gentle" things—an idyllic experience in prospect for all. There was moderate participation in the event—two hundred students or so gathered on the South Oval. I had been a bit uneasy during the day, because I well knew how one thing could lead to another, but the afternoon passed quietly into evening, and I had a relaxed feeling as your Aunt Cleo and I went to our room on the southeast corner of the second floor of the president's house, to listen to the ten-o'clock news on television and then get a good night's sleep.

But I had evaluated the day prematurely. I had not taken the Loyal Knights of Old Trusty into consideration. The Loyal Knights were members of an honorary engineering fraternity; Old Trusty was a small cannon possessed by the group, which was fired annually—several times—the night preceding Engineering Week. Old Trusty was something of a misnomer for the gun. It had not always been trustworthy in the past; several years earlier it had gone off prematurely and blown the hands off one of its attendants. Perhaps several whose sleep had been disturbed by its late-night booming had other names for it.

Apparently the Loyal Knights of Old Trusty decided that the activities of Gentle Thursday should end on a more vigorous note—or, perhaps, in view of the fact that Engineering Week was approaching (though not for several months), they decided to test their symbol of membership to see whether it was in good working order. In any event, shortly before midnight they took the little cannon to the Tower housing area (Couch Center) and placed it in the center of the three twelve-story buildings and prepared it for firing.

In making their preparations, they may have used too much powder, or possibly the effect was amplified by sound waves bouncing from one tall building to another. Be that as it may, the blast surpassed anything the gun had been known to produce in prior use. It was deafening—reverberating all over town and beyond.

One of the towers housed women; the others, men. The sound woke everyone. Men rushed from their towers to see what was going on, and girls pulled curtains on lighted rooms to get a view. Seeing the growing crowd below, a couple of girls were inspired to seek attention for themselves, and one of them, after gyrating sinuously at a window, started to remove her nightgown, silhouetted by backlighting. Several other girls indulged in provocative antics.

65

All of this aroused the male crowd between the towers below, and someone yelled "Panty raid!"

We had had panty raids at OU a couple of times in the past, but the activity had apparently lost favor with the male students. The crowd decided that this was a good time to revive the past, and soon the entire group was yelling "Panty raid!'

By this time the campus police had reached the area, and with the help of counselors from Cross and Wilson centers were able to keep the mob out of the women's housing. Counselors within the women's housing soon got the strip-tease acts under control, but not before they had made a psychological impact on the men below.

Frustrated at the women's tower, the crowd took off for Cate Center, the University's other large housing complex for women, but there too police and counselors were able to keep out the would-be invaders. The crowd then headed for Fraternity-Sorority Row, south of Lindsey Street.

Many sorority houses escaped invasion when their occupants threw bits of lingerie from upstairs windows. But five boys gained entrance to one sorority house through second-story windows and soon emerged with armloads of feminine undergarments while a thousand or so watched from below.

The riot had reached really serious proportions by the time the mob reached another sorority house. They broke down the front door, and more than two hundred students rushed upstairs into the girls' living quarters. Several girls were handled rather roughly. A similar invasion of yet another house was prevented by the intervention of fraternity members who had reached the scene.

Eight students were arrested for unlawful assembly during the melee. Later the police announced that the ones arrested were no more guilty than others but were the only ones they had been able to catch. So much for "Gentle Thursday."

Later, when I was asked by the press why students occasionally behave in this manner, I refused all comment. I had received some mildly adverse publicity after the first panty raid at OU, when I was asked to explain why students could possibly behave in such fashion. I had replied, "I can't explain this mob lust for lingerie." Then I added, unwisely, "When I was in college, such activities were entirely a matter of private enterprise—never group effort." My comment was quoted the next day in the papers, much to my dismay. Your Aunt Cleo didn't like it.

In considering disturbances of this kind, I think that we should realize that, while students come to a university to learn and have experiences that will expedite their maturation, they are likely to be extremely immature in the beginning. Individually or as members of a group, they cannot be expected to have good judgment all the time. It has been said that "good judgment comes from experience, and in turn, experience comes from bad judgment." A university should be a place where bad judgment is expected and can be exercised safely and profitably by students—perhaps even occasionally by faculty and administration.

Critics of a university, especially critics of student behavior, should realize that if those attending an institution already had information and maturity there would be little need for universities. On the other hand, students who receive criticism should receive it philosophically, with the understanding that, in the words of Dr. Edward Eddy, "denunciation of the young is part of the hygiene of older people and greatly assists in the circulation of their blood."

The public should realize, as President W. Allen Wallace, of the University of Rochester, once stressed, that it is difficult to gain an adequate impression of anything by viewing its constituent parts one at a time. He pointed out that an animated electric sign in Times Square might have significance and meaning that one would never suspect by watching just a single one of its bulbs blinking on and off. He added: "Rush Rhees Library, on the George Eastman quadrangle at the University of Rochester, bears on either side of its main portals two inscriptions from which generations of students have drawn inspiration. The inscription to the left of the portals reads: 'Here is a history of human ignorance, error, superstition, folly, war, and waste recorded by human intelligence for the admonition of wiser ages still to come.' The other inscription reads: 'Here is the history of man's hunger for truth, goodness, and beauty leading him slowly on through flesh to spirit, from bondage to freedom, from war to peace.'"

Like the electric sign, a university must be viewed in the broader, overall perspective if the significance of its entire effort is to be understood. Thus an isolated report of a nonviolent student protest on the university campus, such as occurred on your own, taken out of context, might be regarded as near-lawless behavior and a rebellion against legitimate authority. Conversely, explored in proper context, it might be found to be an earnest and effective effort by perceptive and intelligent students to bring about much-needed improvement in the operation of the institution. Of course I find it difficult to relate a panty raid to "earnest and effective effort," but many of the student demonstrations in my experience can, in retrospect, be so related.

In coping with students' problems, try to remember that each individual thinks in terms of his own past experiences. Students think on the basis of very limited experience, but, on the other hand, they have not been victimized by routine or by negative attitudes toward change that often develop with longer living. When they become sufficiently aroused to protest to the administration en masse, there is a problem that needs to be solved. Either the administration needs to right a wrong, or there has been a failure of communication. It is the president's responsibility to see that the situation is explored carefully and corrective action taken. Above all, the president should never retreat to a defensive position because of criticism, but should see that the criticism is examined thoroughly for the germ of truth that might lead to improvement.

My love to the family.

Affectionately,

Student-Faculty Relations

Dear Bill,

I was not surprised to learn that, while your student problems have eased through your meetings with student leaders, you are now concerned with student-faculty relations—problems clustered around students' desire to participate in the formulation of university policy. I consider the latter to be a favorable development; obviously some of your students possess the potential for leadership—leadership that your institution has the responsibility for developing. You will find these strong student leaders useful in helping establish the necessary interaction between the administration and the students that I mentioned in an earlier letter.

On most university campuses students and faculty are frequently at odds. Students tend to think that most faculty members are not greatly interested in their welfare. They may criticize the faculty, often justifiably, for being inaccessible—for poorly kept office hours, broken appointments, inadequate counseling, and even missed classes. This criticism may be related, to some degree at least, with the "publish or perish" policies of many universities. Being human, a member of the faculty may put his own retention, promotion, and tenure above the welfare of students. Under such pressure he will inevitably spend as much time as possible in research and the preparation of manuscripts for publication.

But I suspect that there is another, equally basic but less obvious, reason why students and faculty are not always in agreement. Involved, I think, are the contrasting attitudes of the two groups and the impact these have on certain basic responsibilities of good universities. I will try to explain what I mean.

Your institution has a basic responsibility to serve as a sanctuary for the traditional culture that has developed from ancient times in Western civilization. Down through the ages folkways have been carefully culled, some discarded and others preserved to become our conventions, customs, ethics, and standards for human attitudes and behavior. Continued observance of the surviving folkways, because they were considered conducive to the welfare of society, finally gave them the force of law. Indeed, many of them have been incorporated into our formal legal code. In this way our mores and laws were established. The public expects, and may demand, that a state-supported university protect and perpetuate the mores and laws thus established.

But there is a suggestion of orthodoxy in this approach that, carried to the extreme, is unrealistic. There is no leeway for change. The public has forgotten or does not realize that change has occurred in the past—that folkways once accepted are continuously discarded in response to changing human situations. Much of the public may not realize that change is inevitable—that only the rate and kind of change are subject to human control, and these perhaps to only a somewhat limited extent.

Because change is inevitable, a good university must serve as a launching pad for new ideas. This will involve the need to examine and perhaps modify values that have been established by society. Such examination must include the gamut of mores and laws. It follows that in meeting these responsibilities to examine critically, a good university will frequently find itself in the difficult position of questioning the values that it is supposed to preserve—a paradoxical situation—before a public which, not understanding the universal responsibility implied in the term "university," may be suspicious and critical of what it perceives to be going on in the institution.

With few exceptions faculties are preponderantly conservative. While they may not resist change, they are usually willing to preserve the status quo; in fact, they have a tendency to demand that the status quo be preserved in regard to university curricula, policies, and procedures. However, this conservatism is often masked from the public by the publicity given a very few innovative and aggressive scholars who thus may be considered radicals.

Back in the 1930s a handful of OU faculty members attended a state meeting on civil rights, and one or two participated in the program. This caused certain of the news media to label the university a "hotbed of communism" and led to accusations that finally resulted in a series of state legislative investigations. While all of this was going on, a high percentage of the faculty members apparently had little if any interest in civil rights and were content merely to have jobs during the Depression years.

In contrast to the faculty, students are likely to be progressive liberals who may wish to push change past acceptable limits. Recent changes in standards of morality resulting in sexual liberation and a threatening decline of the family as the basic social unit provide an example. Of course, this attitude toward accelerated change is not limited to university students; it is a youth movement. You are aware that I retired early from the OU presidency to go into the banking business. During the past fifteen years I have been amazed by the increasing numbers of unmarried couples (male and female) who open joint checking and savings accounts over the same address at the bank where I spend my mornings. I have known of only one elderly couple who had such accounts.

On Student-Faculty Relations

You will recall that the youth-versus-age confrontation reached a zenith during the sixties, the decade of campus confrontations. During that stretch of time persons under twenty-five generally considered those over thirty to be approaching senility, and certainly untrustworthy in judgment or motive. Those over thirty tended to regard those under twenty-five as anarchists or fools or both. Neither view was entirely correct, though, of course, there was a modicum of truth in each. During that decade I recall taking comfort in the encouraging thought that those under twenty-five would one day become over thirty.

Perhaps the most vigorous advocates of change during the sixties were the members of the Students for a Democratic Society. This group believed in absolute democracy— no authority was to be vested in anyone. One day four members of the organization visited my office to discuss their views and beliefs. They assured me that there was no hope for the future of the country unless all existing institutions were destroyed and a fresh start was made. The youth of the land must have charge of the reconstruction, and everything would be done in a democratic way, with no one having power over anyone else.

As an illustration of the organization's democracy, they told me that, when the local chapter met, there was no chairman because a chairman would have, at least some control of the meeting. When I asked them if they thought the country could be run with all the citizens being equal and no one authorized to give instructions, they answered in a vigorous affirmative. I then asked them how, under such circumstances, food could arrive at Chicago and other metropolitan centers with no one authorized to order it sent. After a brief pause, one of them answered: "Well, President Cross, we just know what is wrong with the country. We don't know exactly what to do about it, but we know that something must be done and that nothing being done will work!"

While the tensions of the sixties, followed by the anti-war demonstrations of the seventies, have passed, there are still divergences of views between youth and age at practically all institutions of higher learning that need to be reconciled, or at least lessened, if the institutions are to provide optimal educational opportunities for the students.

Establishing a proper balance in the university's responsibilities to serve as a sanctuary for traditional culture and at the same time provide a launching pad for new ideas is not easy. The faculty to some extent and certainly the public from which the institution receives its financial support often exert pressure to preserve the traditional culture. On the other hand, the students, whom the institution was established to serve, may apply equal or even greater pressure to institute what may appear to be radical and even revolutionary changes.

You are likely to receive much gratuitous advice about what should be done in your institution. From the public you may receive communications urging the application of whatever disciplinary measures may be necessary to bring the students into line. Fortunately in recent years such pressure has lessened. But I suspect that you will become increasingly aware of student agitation for a greater voice in institutional affairs, demands that students must have the right to establish their own regulations and rules of conduct, or even the right to play a dominant role in the development of courses, curricular patterns, and other matters.

I think you will agree that the problem cannot be solved through any effort of the older to suppress the younger, or from the effort of the younger to seize power from the older. The solution must come from the development of a working partnership of the two groups wherein efforts are made to reach decisions through dialogues, discussions, and mutual understanding.

I think I made a step toward a solution of such problems during my presidency of OU by giving students representation on all university committees and creating student councils that were associated with the major administrative posts of the institution. I added students to all committees appointed from my office—even to the search committees set up to fill deanships or to name other administrative officials. I persuaded the deans and other administrative personnel to organize councils with which they met periodically. You may want to try this.

Working together as partners, the students, faculty, and administration can shape the university and thereby assure themselves of significant roles in shaping the far-reaching social, economic, and cultural changes that inevitably will come in the wake of the great technological changes that have been and are taking place. Through such cooperative effort these segments of the university can become coarchitects of the future, rather than merely passive recipients of whatever the future may bring.

Through an educational partnership of this nature the older and the younger may learn to live more easily and harmoniously with each other. After practicing on each other for a while, both may learn to live easily and harmoniously with other people, first at home and then abroad. In the process some of them may become inclined to resist the very prevalent neurotic desire to dominate, control, or exploit others and come to realize that ultimately each individual finds it more satisfying to give of his talents in the service of others than to acquire power over them.

I realize that all of this may sound a bit idealistic to you, but widespread realization that service to others can bring the best possible fulfillment in life is the world's greatest need. The impact of such a realization could lead to peaceful living—something rarely found today at any level, from families to nations. Naturally, I would like to see your university become involved with the effort to bring this about.

Affectionately,

On Official Guests

Dear Bill,

It must have been an interesting and pleasant experience to have the French ambassador as a house guest last week! I am sure that Michelle, who, as I recall, is majoring in French, enjoyed the opportunity to test her linguistic accomplishments.

Your account of the visit produced nostalgic remembrance of similar visitations in the president's home at OU. During the 1940s hotels and motels were lacking in Norman. It was necessary to house distinguished visitors either in Oklahoma City—a decided inconvenience—or in the guest room in the president's house. There were two bedrooms in the old Faculty Club Building, which was just north and west of the president's house—almost in its backyard—but these quarters were inadequate for guests, poorly furnished and lacking of service. Your Aunt Cleo and I knew this from firsthand experience, because we had spent our first night in Norman there when we arrived from South Dakota in late August of 1934.

Realizing the bad impression the rooms would make on visitors, Joe Brandt, who succeeded William Bennett Bizzell as president of OU, remodeled a room on the second floor of the president's house for official guests of the university. Perhaps it would be more accurate to say that his wife, Sallye, remodeled it. At any rate she received some unwarranted criticism for spending state money on the project. Thereafter, a series of interesting and important guests occupied the room.

During the summer of 1945 the Earl of Halifax (Edward Frederick Lindley Wood), the British ambassador to the United States and Lady Halifax visited Oklahoma City, and we persuaded the distinguished diplomat and his lady to spend some time at the University, where he gave a speech to a large audience in the Union Ballroom. As usual, the guestroom in the president's house was made available to them.

At the end of the day, our guests, weary from the busy schedule that had been arranged for them, retired to their room a half hour or so before Cleo and I went upstairs. Passing their room as we went down the hall, we were a little startled to see two pairs of shoes outside their door. Obviously they had assumed that shoe-shining service was included with the hospitality. We certainly had no houseboy to whom such duties could be delegated, and Bill, at nine, was too young to be entrusted with the responsibility; this was a matter of international importance. I am sure that you already have guessed the outcome. Fortunately, both pairs of shoes were black. Using a can of partly dried-out polish, I was able to bring them to what I considered a brilliant sheen—"spit and polish"—of which any army private facing company inspection would have been envious, while Cleo watched—laughing.

A year or two ago, while reminiscing before a student group, Cleo inaccurately reported that "we" shined the Halifax shoes. Her only contribution was to supply dubious vocal encouragement and some criticism.

Although I am sure that Lord and Lady Halifax were pleased by the appearance of their shoes, they did not leave a tip for the houseboy. They were, however, very gracious in expressing appreciation for the courtesies they had received.

There were, of course, many notable visitors to the president's house during the nearly twenty-five years that we lived there. Early in 1958 the members of the Young Democrats Club of the University decided that the twenty-fifth anniversary of Franklin Delano Roosevelt's first inauguration should be celebrated on the campus. The members of the student committee and their faculty adviser were able to persuade Eleanor Roosevelt and former President Harry S. Truman to speak at a huge banquet that they were planning for March 4 in the Union Ballroom. It was difficult for me to believe that they could accomplish this, but Cleo and I readily approved their suggestion that Mrs. Roosevelt have the guestroom in the president's house. We did not have room for President Truman but this posed no problem, they said, because a long-term friend in Oklahoma City had offered his home. As we learned later, however, Truman was not about to be "looked after." He sent word that he would stay in the Lockett Hotel in Norman—by then Norman had a hotel.

Mrs. Roosevelt and President Truman arrived at Will Rogers Airport, in Oklahoma City, on different flights during the midmorning of March 4. They were met by an entourage of Young Democrats and various political dignitaries, including June Benson, mayor of Norman, and Governor Raymond Gary. I was on hand to meet Harry, but I did not wait for Eleanor's plane; I hurried back to Norman so I would be there to greet the former first lady when she arrived at the president's house.

A spring shower was falling in Norman that day. Soon Mrs. Roosevelt's car and several others pulled up on Boyd Street in front of the house, where several dozen individuals were assembling to witness the arrival, in defiance of the rain. It was a rather long walk from the street to the house, and I tried to reach the car in time to tell Eleanor's escorts to take her car to the back of the house, where she could leave the car under a porte-cochere and avoid getting wet.

But I was too late; she was already on the brick walk that led to the front door. Dressed in a black coat, black hat, and white scarf and adorned with a corsage given her by the Norman Camp Fire Girls, she huddled under two umbrellas held by very attentive students and slowly made her way up the brick walk to the columned shelter over the entrance to the house. There, with wet feet and damp clothing, she paused for a few minutes while Mayor Benson made her an honorary citizen of Norman. By this time Truman was seen making his way up the walk, and he, too, was given honorary Norman citizenship. I can still see Harry standing in the entrance to the house—very erect, with birdlike visage and smiling broadly. Harry left almost immediately with an enthusiastic student escort to explore the university—including the library, the law school, and, in the afternoon, the football stadium, where Bud Wilkinson had spring practice well under way.

Mrs. Roosevelt, as was to be expected, was a most gracious and considerate guest. A hitch in the arrangements immediately developed, however. She had brought her secretary with her, and she asked us to give her a room as close as possible to her own. Cleo and I were taken aback, because no mention had been made of the secretary; more important, we did not have an extra room—only a sleeping porch with several single beds at the west end of the second floor.

The problem was solved by moving Braden from his room, between the guestroom and our own, to the sleeping porch. This arrangement satisfied everyone except, possibly, Braden, and he made no perceptible objection. The only flaw in the solution was that Braden, a long-term admirer of General Eisenhower, had a huge framed poster of the general—then the President— on the west wall of his room, placed so that Ike was gazing down on the bed. If I had been sufficiently alert, I could have slipped upstairs and removed the picture before the secretary reached the room; unfortunately I had forgotten all about the picture.

It was soon apparent why Eleanor needed her secretary with her. Immediately after she was settled in her room, she began work, dictating segments of her syndicated column, "My Day."

She worked until shortly before three o'clock, when she was taken to a press conference in the Union Building, followed by a reception in the Faculty Club. Back at the house about 5:30, she spent some time with her secretary and then made preparations for the dinner.

After she was dressed for the occasion and we were about ready to leave the house, she discovered that one of the straps of her slip had come loose. Cleo offered to sew the strap back in place. Eleanor said no, that would not be necessary; all she needed was a safety pin to pin strap and slip together. During the dinner Cleo and I talked briefly about the great lady's imperturbable handling of the situation.

Eleanor was principal speaker that evening, but there was an impressive number of speeches by other political luminaries, including Governor Gary; Oklahoma's Senators Mike Monroney and Bob Kerr; Paul Butler, the Democratic national chairman; and, of course, former President Truman.

An overflow crowd estimated at thirteen hundred was waiting when we arrived at the ballroom (the overflow watched the program on television in the Ming Room, the Union restaurant).

The preliminary speakers devoted their time largely to praise of Franklin Delano Roosevelt and the virtues of the Democratic party at the expense of the Eisenhower administration. If Roosevelt was there in spirit, as an empty chair at the speaker's table implied, he doubtless enjoyed the occasion immensely.

Thunderous applause greeted the introduction of Harry S. Truman. Harry spent his time reviewing the careers of past presidents and made no disparaging remarks about Eisenhower. His optimistic suggestion at one point that, because of the effective efforts of President Roosevelt, future wars might be avoided caught my attention.

A second thunderous standing ovation greeted the presentation of Eleanor Roosevelt. She discussed her husband's achievements in ending the Depression and spoke of the country's international obligations of the future. She pointed out that the main challenge to our country was not a military one and that the real solution to world problems must be economic, cultural, and spiritual.

We were back home by about 11:30. Eleanor soon went to the guestroom, and her secretary to Braden's room. Cleo and I wondered how the secretary would enjoy sleeping under President Eisenhower's searching gaze. But she was there only briefly. At six o'clock the next morning some Young Democrats arrived to take our distinguished guest and her secretary to the airport, from which their plane was scheduled to depart at seven. After Eleanor had gone, Cleo and I agreed that her visit had been one of the truly memorable events of our fourteen-year stay in the president's house.

We were, however, embarrassed by the gracious lady's long walk in the rain from Boyd Street to the front door of the house. We knew that practically no one used the sheltered entrance on the north side. We finally decided that the brick walk up to the house should be removed and a curved driveway installed so that cars could bring guests close to the front door. It appeared that an opportunity to do this would come with the scheduled widening and resurfacing of Boyd Street, after which parking would be prohibited on Boyd in that block. Although we regretted the city's plan to cover the brick paving on Boyd with asphalt, we were glad to have an excuse to build the curved driveway. For some time the new driveway was called Eleanor Roosevelt Drive, in honor of her visit.

Another occasion that proved memorable, though in a different way, was the visit of Carl Sandburg, who came to the university in the late 1940s to give a public address. All of us were captivated by this renowned Lincoln historian and writer of stories for children. He was one of the most kindly men I have ever known; Cleo and Mary-Lynn characterized him as "sweet." The high point in his visit with us came at breakfast the morning after he gave his address. When Cleo asked him what he would like for breakfast, he replied, "Only oatmeal and coffee." While the oatmeal was being prepared, Sandburg and I chatted in the little breakfast room at the west end of the house. Braden, who was about three and a half, was up and in action—wandering about carrying a box of Cheerios. The boy had early developed a liking for Cheerios. He ate them as one would eat popcorn, without milk or sugar. His mother kept him provided with a box, which he stored with his toys—always available for munching when he felt the need.

Sandburg's oatmeal was finally ready, and he settled himself at the table to have breakfast. As he was picking up the cream pitcher, Braden came in and proffered his box of Cheerios, thrusting it up into Sandburg's lap. Sandburg briefly looked puzzled and then, glancing in my direction said, "Oh, he wants to share his Cheerios with me. Thank you very much, Braden." He took the box of Cheerios— into which a grubby little hand had been thrust frequently —and shook a goodly amount of its contents over his oatmeal. Then, after adding appropriate amounts of cream and sugar, he ate the contents of the bowl to the last spoonful.

Breakfast was over before nine o'clock, and Sandburg's plane was not scheduled to leave Will Rogers Airport until sometime after noon. Hoping to make his last hours with us as enjoyable as possible, I asked him if he would like to have a bird's-eye view of the university and its environs from the institution's recently acquired Beechcraft Bonanza. He instantly agreed, and we were off for Westheimer Field. It was a beautiful morning, clear of clouds and turbulence, and we spent the better part of an hour examining the university from an altitude of a thousand feet or so and then circled Tinker Air Force Base—counterclockwise, so that our guest could have a view of Oklahoma City. We ended the trip by flying west to Will Rogers Airport, thence to the Canadian River, and finally back to Westheimer.

During the flight Sandburg showed more interest in natural terrain than he did in the things man had placed there. He was much interested in the fact that Norman was situated on the line where the forests of the East give way to the grasslands of the West.

Finally, back at the house, he went to the guestroom to prepare for his departure. I told him to let me know when he had finished packing and I would bring his luggage downstairs. But in a few minutes he appeared, coming down the steps. He was carrying his bag in one hand and a book in the other. After thanking us for our hospitality, he gave the book to Braden as he left the house. It was a copy of his *Rootabaga Stories.* On the flyleaf he had written, "For Braden Cross, with good wishes and thanks for his company at breakfast before riding in a Beechcraft. Carl Sandburg— 1949." Braden, who is now practicing anesthesiology in Norman and has a three-year-old boy of his own, claims to have a dim remembrance of Sandburg's visit. Beyond any doubt, however, the autographed book is the most treasured item in his library.

I hope all of this hasn't bored you. It would appear that I have again been overpowered by nostalgia.

Affectionately,

On Faculty Organization

Dear Bill,

It may be scant comfort, but you are by no means the first university president to become concerned about his school's obsolete curricula and occasional uninspired teaching. You will recall that during the 1960s student criticism of curricular obsolescence and nonrelevant course content was rampant on university campuses. As far as I can tell, the criticism brought very little improvement, though apparently some course changes have been made on some campuses, mainly the addition of courses on minority cultures. For the most part changes in curricular patterns, course content, and teaching techniques have been minuscule.

Almost from the beginnings of American universities faculties have had at least nominal control over all curricular matters. Today, I think it fair to say, faculties are in complete control. That is as it should be, because only the faculties have the competence to make curricular decisions.

The difficulty in bringing about needed changes stems from the fact that faculties are not structured—organized—for change. For example, the faculty of each degree-recommending college at the University of Oklahoma establishes its own curricular requirements for graduation. The departments within the college provide the required courses, supplemented, of course, by courses from the College of Arts and Sciences, but the course content and teaching techniques are controlled by those who do the teaching. No overall committee or other agency of either college or department has the responsibility of studying curricula in the light of social and technological change and making recommendations for corresponding changes that may be needed. Contemporary faculties seem either unaware of the need or unwilling to delegate or deputize their colleagues for such responsibility. With respect to course content and teaching techniques they insist on individual decision; with respect to changes in curricular patterns they seem to prefer that the faculty act as a committee of the whole. As a result, there have been no really significant curricular innovations in higher education during the past four or five decades except for the few, mentioned above, having to do with the history and culture of minority groups.

With the exception of some added programs the only significant curricular change at the University of Oklahoma that I recall since my arrival in 1934 involved the College of Arts and Sciences foreign-language requirement for graduation. But this change was not made by the college faculty. It came as a result of action by the State Board of Regents for Higher Education. With a proliferation of junior colleges in Oklahoma since World War II, none of which required foreign language, complaints concerning the University's requirements came in great abundance when junior-college students entered the University for their final two years of work. The regents, after studying the situation for a while, decided that the junior-college students should be able to transfer to the University without prejudice—that the requirements for the first two years should be the same throughout the state higher-education system. This action—without merit in my judgment—may have signaled a significant change in the extent to which the faculty of the university controls its curricula. Authority to control the curricula for higher education was given to the state regents by constitutional amendment back in the 1940s, but this was the first time the regents exercised the authority except in approving or disapproving recommendations from the institutions comprising the system. It is hoped that the regents do not become addicted to taking such initiative action, but that may well happen because of faculty reluctance to make changes on their own.

Early in my presidency of OU, I became aware of this problem—and several related ones. The basic unit of the institution then, as now, was the department. All faculty members specializing in the same general field of learning, such as English or physics, held membership in the same department. Related departments were grouped together to form schools or colleges (the distinctions between the two were not always clear to me), except that all the nonprofessional departments were included in the College of Arts and Sciences. I should add that not all colleges had departments; examples were the University College and the Graduate College.

A department was administered by a chairman, a school by a director, and a college by a dean. The traditional chain of command ("responsibility" would be a better word) was from department head to director or dean to vice-president and, finally, to the president.

After the academic budget for the school year had been determined, the regents, basing their action on recommendations from the president, divided the budget among the various colleges. Each dean then subdivided the allocation to his college among its departments. The chairman largely determined the use of the departmental funds, though his recommendations concerning faculty salaries had to be approved by the dean, the president, and the regents.

It occurred to me that there were some flaws in this way of doing things. One weakness in the system was that when salaries were based solely on administrative decisions administrators invariably turned up with salaries too high in relation to those of faculty members. It seemed to me also that the deans, who, I thought, had primary responsibility for initiating curricular renovation, spent too much of their time administering fiscal affairs. But the basic problem, I thought, was that through the system the progress of the institution was being limited to the intelligence and imagination of too few people. It provided for too much concentration of power in the offices of certain administrative personnel. Deans of colleges that were comprised of departments had money to divide among the departments. Deans of colleges that did not have departments had no money to divide. Money, rather than knowledge, is power—even on a university campus.

One especially unfortunate aspect of the situation was that the dean of the Graduate College, having no departments under his supervision, also had no voice in such important matters as faculty recruitment, salary increases, and faculty promotions, even though he had the responsibility of developing graduate work and research in the institution.

I decided to experiment with a different plan at the University of Oklahoma. According to the plan, the department was still regarded as the primary academic unit, but related departments were not organized or grouped to form schools and colleges. I had the departments listed alphabetically as departments of the University and not of a college. The departments provided the courses that were used in the programs of study leading to the various degrees granted, but were not controlled by deans.

Under this reorganization the college consisted of a dean and a group of faculty members with related interests who had the joint responsibility of developing and improving programs of study leading to the various degrees. Relieved from the responsibility of supervising departmental affairs,

I thought, each dean could be expected to take the initiative in studying and modernizing the curricula of his college.

The college had no budget except the budget for the office of its dean. It had no authority over departmental budgets, the promotion of departmental personnel, or salary increases for departmental personnel. The dean made recommendations concerning the budgets of departments that provided service courses for his college, but his recommendations did not carry the weight of authority.

The maintenance-and-salary budget request of each department was prepared by a departmental committee and submitted to the entire staff for approval. Copies of the request were then sent to the dean of the undergraduate college in which the departmental staff held membership, the dean of the University College, and the dean of the Graduate College. The deans reviewed the requests thoroughly and independently, added their recommendations, and then passed the budget on to the newly organized Budget Council for study and a recommendation to the president. The Budget Council consisted of members of the faculty nominated to the president by the University Senate, plus the financial vice-president of the University, who acted as chairman. The council, because it had the opportunity to examine carefully the budgets of all departments, was in a position to see that academic funds were equitably distributed. Once a departmental budget had been approved, no dean had any additional influence or authority over it. The department could disburse its maintenance and equipment money as needed, though all salaries had to be approved by the regents.

Recommendations concerning course changes were initiated by the department involved, and recommendations involving curricular changes were initiated within the college and submitted to the college faculty for approval. All such recommendations were sent to another newly organized unit, the Academic Council, for study and approval before being forwarded to the president. Course and curricular changes needed the approval of the regents of the university and, finally, approval of the State Board of Regents for Higher Education.

I am sure you are thinking that these procedures were unduly cumbersome. It's true that they took more time than those followed previously, but through their use I believe far fewer mistakes were made, and the university had the benefit of the considered judgments of all persons most concerned with each area. Budgets of the departments and other matters of departmental importance were not determined by administrative personnel until recommendations had been made by members of the faculty. Each dean had influence, but not power or authority, in keeping with his responsibilities. There were no chains of command, only chains of responsibility.

There are several reasons why the faculty should have virtual control of academic affairs in a university as well as a voice in the formulation of institutional policies. The most important reason, of course, is that the faculty has a great deal to contribute. The collective judgment of a large number of individuals will always be more reliable than the judgment of a few. Then there is the matter of faculty morale. It has been suggested that members of the faculty will be more contented and satisfied and, therefore, do better work if they know that they have a voice in the affairs of their institution. I suspect that this assumption has some validity. I know of several faculty members who stayed at the University of Oklahoma, though offered higher salaries elsewhere, because they felt that at OU they would have some voice in directing the destiny of the institution. OU's great physicist Jens Rud Nielsen on several occasions was offered nearly double the salary that he was receiving at OU. He stayed, I believe for that reason.

I should emphasize, however, that absolute democracy may be undesirable on a university campus. Moreover, it may not be desirable to have a completely contented faculty. I suspect that, to a very large extent, past improvement in higher education has been brought about through the discontent of faculties. Of course, it must be intelligent and constructive discontent. I should add that I think one of the worst things that can happen in a university is for the faculty to develop complete confidence in the administration. And this may happen if the administration insists upon completely democratic procedures. Under such conditions the faculty may become lazy and disinclined to participate in the meetings, conferences, and committee work incumbent upon members of a democracy of any kind. At best, committees do not work rapidly, and their efforts can become desultory. You will recall the old saying that if Moses had been a committee the Children of Israel would still be in Egypt. Probably the best situation that can develop in an institution of higher learning is the one in which the faculty harbors a mild but definite suspicion of the administration. It goes without saying that the suspicion should be unjustified.

Part of the system that I developed at OU still survives. Departments have been returned to membership in colleges, and the undergraduate deans have regained some measure of control over budgets. Even so, recommendations are still originated by committees, and at least three deans, rather than one, are involved in the approval of departmental recommendations. I must confess however, that the reorganizations I brought about did not result in any systematic planning for curricular revision or renovation. The only significant changes at OU were brought about through pressure from minority groups to include new ethnic courses and programs of study.

Good luck as you struggle with these problems.

Affectionately,

On Personnel Retention—Salaries

January 15

Dear Bill,

Many would agree, I think, that one of the sore spots in faculty-administration relationships is the salary differentials that exist in practically all institutions. Administrators, at least upper-level administrators, prevailingly receive higher salaries than those of all but the most distinguished members of the faculty. This is true, I suppose, because the public seems to revere administrative and managerial skills—possibly because in our materialistic culture profits are the measure of success, and profits accrue as the result of skilled management. This idea apparently has spilled from the business and industrial world over into the educational world—an unfortunate development because, in a university, the really important work is done by the faculty.

Long before I became president of OU, I became aware that the best salaries were paid to the administrative personnel. The fact was discussed frequently and critically during coffee breaks at the Union Building. When I assumed the presidency, I quickly discovered the extent of the inequity. I found that the most distinguished member of the faculty received much less pay than the weakest of the deans. At that time (1944) the salaries of full professors ranged from about $2,000 to $3,800 for nine months' service. The chairman of a department received at least two or three hundred dollars more a year than the best professor in his department—in some instances as much as $4,000 a year. The range for deans was from $4,500 to $6,000, with the deans of law and medicine receiving the latter amount. Salaries of members of the teaching faculty as a whole were so low that their only hope of receiving a living wage was to secure an administrative position of some kind—a departmental chairmanship or a deanship.

Under such circumstances it is easy to understand why many members of the teaching faculty envied the administrators and developed ambitions to become administrators themselves. It seemed to me that several members of the faculty had become so involved in campus political activity directed toward the securing of administrative appointments that they were giving minimum attention to the jobs they had been hired to do. This, of course, subverted the main function of the university—the teaching and counseling of students and research.

I became convinced that some remedial action was needed. Why should an internationally known professor in the physics department be paid a paltry $3,800 a year, while a dean not well known even in his own state received $5,000? Clearly, I thought, steps should be taken to place greater emphasis on teaching, counseling, and research and less emphasis on administration. As a first step in this direction I recommended to the regents that we eliminate the differential between salaries of departmental chairmen and full professors. The regents approved my recommendation that departmental chairmen no longer receive extra compensation for performing administrative duties but receive only a reduction in teaching load.

This change decreased—even minimized—the importance of being appointed to a chairmanship—a favorable result, because chairmen were appointed for a specific term (four years) under a plan initiated by my predecessor, Joe Brandt, when he came to the University in 1941. While it was possible for a chairman to be reappointed, in effect the position was up for grabs every four years in each department, and, by playing politics effectively with the dean, any member of a departmental staff could hope to receive the appointment. Minimizing the importance of the departmental chairmanship reduced such political activity to some extent.

At that time the deans had a free hand in selecting the chairmen of departments within their colleges. Of course, these appointments required the approval of the president and the regents of the University, but it had been the custom to accept the deans' recommendations without question. I decided to experiment with a different procedure—one that would prevent the deans from rewarding political henchmen with appointments. Under the reorganization I mentioned in my last letter, departments were reorganized as basic units of the University rather than the colleges. At the time the reorganization was put into effect, it was easy to change the method of selecting departmental administrators. I decided that the president should be involved directly in naming the chairmen.

It seemed advisable to give the staff of each department a voice in selecting its chairman. I thought it unwise to have the staff elect its administrator, because that would increase the political maneuvering on the campus. But I did have each staff select a representative who would come to my office to discuss the appointment with me. The representative was asked to explain his or her responsibilities to each associate in the department and bring the names of two or three members whom the majority of the staff would find acceptable. After receiving the representative's report, I would discuss the list of names with the deans of the University College, the undergraduate college most closely involved with the department, and the Graduate College. We would agree on who should be named.

I should emphasize, I suppose, that I did not make these changes without consulting the Faculty Senate. I did not ask the Senate for a recommendation but merely presented the matter to the members at one of their monthly sessions. I knew that the plan would have their approval, because it meant greater democracy on the campus, but even so, faculties do not like to have such decisions announced by fiat.

I should add that this new arrangement appeared to work exceptionally well. With the exception of a very few isolated cases, friction between departmental chairmen and members of the teaching staffs virtually disappeared.

To bring about better relationships between deans and faculties, whenever it was necessary to name a new dean, I invited the faculty of the college to work with me in the selection process through the use of a selections committee. The members of the committee were elected by the faculty of the college involved. I had a feeling that the faculty, having had a voice in the selection of the dean, would take a paternal interest in the new appointee and cooperate in his or her success. Conversely, the new dean, knowing that the faculty had had a prominent voice in the choice, might, through a feeling of appreciation, come into the situation with a better attitude toward the faculty. This plan worked very successfully, in my opinion. Of course, selections committees are now widely used in the procurement of university personnel, but I have the impression that the committees are now too heavily loaded with administrators and, on some occasions, regents. The faculty should be strongly represented on all such committees.

In a further effort to encourage effective faculty effort at OU, special professorships were created for a few who had performed exceptionally well in either teaching or research. Because faculty members might achieve distinction in one of these activities with less success in the other, two categories of professorships were established. For those who chose to devote their lives to superior teaching and counseling of students, thus having little time for research or other creative effort, we created the David Ross Boyd Professorships (named for the first president of the University of Oklahoma). For those who were unusually productive in research and publication the Research Professorships were created.

When these special professorships were created, the salaries were based on the average salaries paid to the deans of the University. The nine-month stipends for David Ross Boyd professors and research professors were set at the average salaries paid deans for twelve months. This meant that the holders of special professorships would receive a higher monthly salary than that of the deans, and, because they almost invariably had summer employment, their annual salaries were markedly higher than those of the deans. Of course, we were very careful in awarding these professorships; usually no more than four or five were awarded in each category in any academic year.

The results of this plan were, for the most part, what I had hoped for. Exceptionally talented members of the faculty lost their ambitions to become administrators; a David Ross Boyd professorship or a research professorship became their objective. The first stipends of $5,000 for nine months' service paid the recipients of the appointments were 25 percent higher than the highest salaries paid other professors and were equal to the salaries paid all the deans except the deans of law and medicine.

While I was cheered by this development, my satisfaction was tempered by the fact that the salaries for the special professorships were no more than equal to the average salaries paid all professors in many institutions with which we had to compete for talent, including such nearby schools as the Universities of Missouri, Texas, Kansas, and Colorado. While the new salaries might be effective in holding established members of our faculty, we had a rather impressive number of younger faculty members who had great promise but who could not yet be given the distinguished appointments. By using great care in recruiting, we were able to bring to the campus many young men and women with exceptional potential who, after spending a few years with us, would be lured to better-financed institutions. Our faculty was being constantly skimmed of talent, and, to use wartime parlance, the university was operating as an "academic boot camp."

The situation finally became so serious that we decided that something must be done. It occurred to us that a possible solution might be a plan to supplement the salaries of our best young faculty members with money obtained from private sources. Perhaps after the university had paid promising young faculty as much as the traffic would bear from appropriated funds, supplements could be given from private money without causing too much resentment from those not so favored. I explored the idea with certain industrial leaders of the state, and received encouragement. The Halliburton Oil Company, of Duncan, Oklahoma, immediately agreed to provide a supplement for a promising young professor in the College of Engineering.

All of this finally led to a campaign called the "Plan for Excellence." Over a five-year period (1962-67), we raised approximately $18 million from business, industry, and other private contributions within the state and beyond. Using these funds as supplements to state-paid salaries, we were able to stem the flow of talent from the University, and the quality of our faculty gradually increased.

I realize that I may seem to have wandered from your immediate problem—curricular obsolescence and inadequate classroom teaching and counseling. Yet, basic to the success of any university is the quality of its faculty. To attract a good faculty, the university must offer adequate salaries.

With reasonably good quality at hand, it is up to the university administration to provide the leadership and stimulation necessary to inspire superior performance. How this is brought about will differ from institution to institution. In my opinion, however, basic to any such attempt is finding a way to assure the faculty that it will have a voice in determining the destiny of an institution.

Affectionately,

On Fund Raising

January 30

Dear Bill,

The financial problems you describe exist to some degree in every quality university in the country, regardless of the size of the school's budget. Every good institution is always short of funds. In the words of Harold W. Stoke, in *The American College President* (published by Harper & Brothers), the college president who understands this may save himself some psychological problems. He must learn to "accept the fact that he is on a fiscal treadmill, destined always to approach, but never to arrive at the promised land." Stoke states further that a president "may be as successful with donors as was President Hopkins of Dartmouth, or with legislators, as was President Sproul of the University of California, but, nevertheless, the horizon is never reached—it merely recedes."

Further, a president should never expect gratitude from his faculty for the money he obtains from public or private sources; such is expected of him. He may be able to ease the tension between his office and the faculty by securing substantial gifts or appropriations, but he should never expect to see the time when he can relax in comfort and reflect on his situation with complacency. As Stoke points out, "New levels of expenditures are always quickly accepted; salary increases are regarded merely as justice, usually overdue, and a new building provided for chemistry makes, by contrast, biology's needs still more glaring." Enthusiasm generated by increases in budgets and salaries improves the ambience of a campus for a brief period (usually about two weeks)—"like snow upon the desert's dusty face, brightens

101

for a little hour, and is gone" (with apologies to Omar Khay-yám).

Although all of this may not be comforting to the president, there may be good in it for the institution. It has been said that faculty members who, over an extended period of time, are satisfied with their situations, who do not think that they need additional money for research and improved teaching aids, are lacking in imagination. Those who do not think that they deserve promotions and higher salaries may lack the self-confidence and innovative instincts necessary to do their jobs well. Most of the progress made in higher education during the first three-quarters of the twentieth century probably can be related to faculty discontent—discontent expressed constructively. In any event, during my tenure as president of OU, I was continuously plagued by the thought that sufficient funds were not available to take advantage of the innovative potential of our best faculty members.

I am glad that you are making plans to breathe new life into your private-fund-raising program. The fact that you do not have a formal organization with this responsibility—a trust or foundation independent of your university—should cause no undue concern, though you should proceed immediately to develop something of this kind. Probably most state colleges given university status following World War II, like yours, faced similar problems.

To meet this need at OU, we organized the University of Oklahoma Foundation back in the mid-1940s. The foundation was established as a trust fund with, in the beginning, three ex officio trustees: the president of the university, the president of the Alumni Association, and the president of the University Dad's Association. The bylaws, however, provided for a minimum of eight additional trustees, to be elected by donors to the fund as soon as there was a list of contributors large enough to make an election possible. Each donor of $100 or more received a voting certificate entitling him to one vote for each $100 contributed. This ensured that donors of larger gifts would have a proportionate voice in the proper investment and disposition of the resources of the foundation. Independent of the university, the trust declaration gave the trustees broad powers to receive and administer, for the benefit of the university, cash, securities, real estate, endowments, and property of any other kind.

In the beginning our operation was a modest one, conducted largely by the staff in the president's office. I kept the foundation records in my desk. As time went on, and we were able to secure enough donors to enlarge our group of trustees, Boyd Gunning, secretary of the OU Alumni Association was made director of the foundation; he held the dual appointment for the next many years, during which a foundation staff was developed.

I should warn you that it takes a great deal of time and sustained effort by the president to develop a good fund-raising program. In the early stages you will have to do practically all of the work yourself, because prospective donors will not be impressed by anyone other than the head man of the institution. Even after you have your organization completed and operating smoothly, you will still find it necessary to be involved personally when larger gifts are sought. In an earlier letter I mentioned OU's "Plan for Excellence." Before we launched this drive in 1962, I recall discussing its probable success with a member of my governing board. He told me that it would be successful only if I could find the time for personal calls on prospective donors. He was right.

It may be helpful for me to tell you a bit about how this first drive, designed to raise an impressive amount of money, was handled. The plan called for the raising of $20 million over the five-year period from mid-1962 to mid-1967.

We began the drive in Norman, because we knew that we had to demonstrate local support before we could enlist the interest of individuals, businesses, and industries removed from the campus.

Our first targets were the three Norman banks. We reasoned that they had profited greatly from the presence of the University and should be correspondingly receptive to a plan that would result in the institution's further growth and development. It seemed reasonable to me that each bank might be persuaded to contribute $25,000 payable over a five-year period. However, word that the banks would be approached got out before we had done any soliciting, and I soon heard that two of the banks had determined that $5,000 would be a proper contribution. I decided to call on the third bank first to see whether I could obtain a pace-setting contribution closer to the $25,000 mark.

Fortunately, a member of the board of directors of the third bank had just completed two terms as regent of the University. He agreed to go with me to call on the president of the bank. It took less than half an hour to persuade the president that his bank should contribute $25,000. The other two banks could not afford to contribute less, and a week or so later the pledges of all three were in hand.

We used the same strategy in Oklahoma City, where two large banks dominated the financial world. The goal there was $100,000 from each bank. It was difficult to decide which of the two large banks might have the more generous board of directors, but we finally made a decision, and after an hour's session with the bank president, and another hour with the board, we secured a $100,000 pledge. The other large bank was easily persuaded to match the pledge, and the smaller banks came through also, though with smaller amounts. Smaller pledges were subsequently received from several banks in Tulsa, and within a few weeks the total was nearly a half million dollars.

It then seemed time to approach the larger industrial corporations in the state. The most likely prospect, it appeared, was the Phillips Petroleum Corporation, headquartered at Bartlesville, despite the fact that the top executive officers of that company were graduates of the University of Kansas. I called Boots Adams, the president of Phillips, and got permission to appear before the company's executive committee. I think that the story of what happened at that meeting is well worth telling.

Boyd Gunning and I flew to Bartlesville on the chosen day, were met at the airport by a Phillips car, and finally found ourselves in session with six members of the Phillips executive committee, including three graduates of the University of Kansas and one alumnus of the University of Oklahoma, John Houchin (Houchin was destined to become a regent of the University in 1963).

I explained to the committee in careful detail what our fund drive was all about. I emphasized that what we had in mind was a marked improvement in the quality of the OU faculty. The salaries that could be paid from appropriated monies simply were not large enough to attract and hold a high-quality faculty. We needed a core of exceptional individuals around whom we could build. To secure this quality, we proposed to pay the maximum salary the university could afford and then add one or more "supplements" from private money. It was expected, I explained, that a supplement would be $5,000. One supplement, or, in extraordinary cases, two supplements, added to what the university could pay from appropriated money would enable us to hold our best faculty members and occasionally add an exceptional individual.

After I had finished my presentation, I invited discus-

105

sion. Immediately Boots Adams came through: "This makes good sense to me. How much do you think Phillips should contribute?"

The question caught me completely by surprise. I had thought that I was simply giving the executive committee something to think about—that we would talk later about the amount; I had not expected getting down to specifics so soon.

Disconcerted by the directness of Adams's question, I replied, "Well, perhaps a million dollars." And then I made a serious blunder; I added, "Surely not less than a half million." Adams quickly agreed: "A half million seems reasonable to me," adding, "John Houchin, an OU graduate, has meant a great deal more than a half million dollars to Phillips Petroleum." He then asked if there were any comments from the other members of the executive committee.

One member of the committee, a University of Kansas graduate, said, "Well, it does seem that President Cross has come up with a good idea and that Phillips should contribute. But perhaps we should take some time and discuss how much should be given." To this Adams replied, "Hell, we're all here. If the amount needs discussion, let's discuss it." For some reason, there was no further discussion, and Adams told me that Phillips would pledge $500,000 to be given over a five-year period. I sat there kicking myself mentally for having mentioned a half million dollars after I had originally suggested one million. It was clear to me that I could have secured the million dollars as easily as the half-million. The moral here, I think, is that you should never ask for too little when you are dealing with corporate executives. They are used to thinking in larger amounts than those most university personnel deal with, and they are inclined to be skeptical of requests for smaller amounts when large projects are in prospect.

On Fund Raising

Before leaving the meeting, I asked Adams whether it would be all right to tell other prospects what Phillips had pledged. He replied: "I don't want this pledge publicized. I don't want every other school in the area coming and asking for money." I explained that I had no intention of publicizing the generous contribution but that I had an appointment the next week with the president of a certain oil company with headquarters in Houston, Texas. Could I tell him of the Phillips pledge? Adams, apparently acquainted with the name I mentioned, replied, "You tell that son of a bitch that Phillips contributed a million dollars, and if you get a million from him, we'll make our pledge a million also."

I didn't do nearly as well in Houston. I ran into the question, "Why should industry contribute money to publicly supported institutions, when private institutions need the support?" As a matter of fact, I ran into this question every time I approached the president of a corporation—with the exception of Phillips Petroleum.

My answer, which I gave countless times, was simply that, in my view, since the end of World War II there had been very little difference between public and private institutions insofar as sources of funds were concerned. Huge research grants of federal money to the more prominent private schools, such as Yale, Harvard, MIT, and Cal Tech, had in effect made them publicly supported institutions. On the other hand, all the great state universities had become great only because of the private money that they were able to raise to supplement state appropriations. I was able to back up my statement with figures showing the amounts of public funds that had gone to private institutions in recent years and the degree to which public universities had amassed endowment funds.

In spite of these arguments, supported by figures, I found industry slow to accept the idea that corporations should contribute to the University of Oklahoma. But despite this handicap, OU was able to raise approximately $18 million of the $20 million goal during its five-year drive. Boyd Gunning was largely responsible for the success of the drive. After our initial efforts it was he who arranged the schedule of solicitations and planned the travel. All that I had to do was go along and explain the plan.

I tell you all of this to emphasize that there is no way you can raise much money for your institution unless you are willing to do the traveling necessary to make the calls. Raising funds for a state institution from private sources is always arduous and sometimes frustrating, but it can be most rewarding also.

Good luck to you as you get under way with your program.

Affectionately,

On the Use of Knowledge

January 31

Dear Bill,

Your question, "What will be the greatest problem faced by higher education during the remainder of the century?" certainly gives me pause, and it is one that, of course, should receive the serious attention of every college and university president. After some thought, I believe that I can spotlight the problem pretty well, but, unhappily, I am unable to offer a solution. The problem is the difficulty of doing what higher education needs to do if it is to meet its responsibilities to the society it serves.

Back in the early 1950s I received a mimeographed questionnaire from an individual who apparently wanted to reform the human race. He said that he planned to write a book based on the answers he received. Many of his queries seemed vague, even a bit incoherent, and, as I continued to read, I had nearly decided to send the materials to what I called my "screwball file" when I noticed two questions that seemed very pertinent. The first was, "What is your institution failing to accomplish that you think it should accomplish?" The second, consisting of two parts was: "If you could tell your son only one thing upon graduation from college, what would you tell him? Does your university tell this to the sons of other men?"

These were impressive questions. They stimulated me to grope for answers, and in the groping I gave considerable thought to what was going on at institutions of higher learning in the country, especially at OU.

At that time the University of Oklahoma had an enrollment of between twelve and fifteen thousand. It was served by a faculty of approximately five hundred and was housed in a physical plant with a replacement value of perhaps $50 million—a modest evaluation because we had not yet experienced the devastating inflation of the sixties and seventies.

Like other good universities, OU had some fine research laboratories, equipped with extremely complicated instruments, in which, I hoped, the limits of knowledge were being extended nearly every day. I recall thinking of our spectroscopy laboratory, wherein was housed an infrared spectrograph with which it was possible to analyze qualitatively and quantitatively the gases on the surface of the sun. As you well know, through the use of a similar instrument the gas helium was discovered on the sun before it was found in Texas—or, for that matter, anywhere else. With such equipment man had determined the materials of which stars are made.

I thought of the many other tools of research accumulated at OU—the electron microscope, with which it was possible to magnify enormously small objects and make photographs of such minute things as the virus that causes polio, and the polarimeter, with which the contents of live steam could be analyzed with amazing accuracy. There were facilities for doing research in practically every field of knowledge. Because of its research OU, like other colleges and universities, had become a vast reservoir of knowledge. I remember some wag saying that this was true because the freshmen bring in so much each year and the seniors take away so little. Be that as it may, the teaching faculty was busily engaged in making the knowledge available to the students. The institution was fulfilling its function of acquiring and disseminating knowledge.

Then I returned to the gentleman's question: "What is your institution failing to accomplish that you think it should accomplish?" It was difficult to construct an answer by study-

110

ing the university alone. A broader perspective had to be obtained; an overall view of our modern times was necessary.

A conspicuous feature of this overall view was immediately apparent. Despite the great increase in numbers of colleges and universities after World War II and the worldwide distribution of these institutions, together with the vast amount of beneficial information they had made available to mankind, in the minds of many of our citizens the future of the human race seemed more uncertain than at any other time in history. The explosion of hydrogen bombs that ended World War II, and the realization that other nations would soon be able to make such bombs, had created a threat of destruction so impressive that many people became unnerved at the mere prospect of further atomic testing.

The basic information necessary to make an atomic bomb was developed in university research laboratories—a significant fact. The destructive use of this knowledge, allegedly made necessary because others had misused knowledge, had led many to conclude that knowledge in itself was not a good thing—that learning was advancing so rapidly that adequate control of its applications had become impossible.

Some thought that this was true only of scientific discoveries like those pertaining to nuclear bombs and that if a moratorium could be placed on scientific research until the social sciences had time to catch up, the problem could be solved. Other, more thoughtful individuals pointed out that that was not a sound deduction, that any kind of knowledge could be used improperly and certain kinds having to do with the social sciences, especially with the fields of psychology, economics, and sociology, might be fully as dangerous as scientific knowledge in the hands of future Hitlers, Mussolinis, or Stalins. There was no way of knowing what information might be used for the degradation or destruction of mankind. It was not knowledge that was dangerous—it was the intent of the user.

Raymond B. Fosdick expressed this thought well in 1948, when, as president of the Rockefeller Foundation, he gave the dedicatory address at the installation of the 200-inch telescope at Mount Palomar. He said: "Unless we can anchor our knowledge to moral purposes, the ultimate result will be dust and ashes—dust and ashes that will bury the hopes and monuments of men beyond recovery. The towering enemy of man is not his science, but his moral inadequacy."

I had been greatly impressed by Fosdick's speech on that historic occasion, and I recalled it while reflecting on the contents of the questionnaire. It appeared that his talk contained the answer to the man's question. The University of Oklahoma, and other institutions like it, had not been doing enough to develop in students the moral and ethical attitudes necessary to ensure that the fruits of our research laboratories and classrooms would be used wisely in human affairs. Apparently too much attention had been given to information—too little to attitudes and values. As Fosdick hinted, the gap between man's morality and his knowledge must be closed if he is to survive. Obviously this was the responsibility of my university and others—a responsibility that was not being met.

This view was bolstered by a statement attributed to Charles A. Lindbergh: "In a competitive world, life and freedom must be backed by strength, but survival has a time dimension which says that power consists of more than strength of arms. Short term survival may depend on the knowledge of nuclear physics and the performance of supersonic aircraft, but long term survival depends alone on the character of man. Our scientific, economic, and military accomplishments are rooted in the human quality which produces them. In the last analysis, all of our knowledge, all of our action, all of our progress, succeed or fail according to their effect on the human body, mind and spirit." It seemed to me that Lindbergh, like Fosdick, had sized up the situation pretty well. Morality was at least as important a factor in man's survival as technical knowledge.

Pondering all of this back in the early 1950s, I thought that here might be the basic problem facing education, especially higher education—bridging the gap between learning and morality might be the key to the survival of our so-called civilization in the threatening technological age that is emerging. I wondered what the University of Oklahoma could do to help solve the problem.

In trying to formulate an answer, I started with the assumption that the good in man outweighs the bad, though pessimists might insist that the difference is usually very slight. If this is true, when an individual fails in an ethical or moral sense, the fault must lie somewhere in the experiences he has had, among which would surely be included his formal educational experiences. All such failures should be of great concern to those who are involved in the education of our youth—the public schools, colleges, and universities that influence our young people during the early years of their lives. What, I wondered, could be done to provide better experiences—experiences that would lead to more constructive thinking, better attitudes and higher ethical standards?

It occurred to me that a start could be made if every department within the university, especially those having to do with professional training, emphasized frequently the moral and ethical aspects of the training for and practice of a profession. The students should be reminded often that educational opportunities had been given to them not that they might be able to compete more successfully with their less fortunate associates in later life but primarily that they might be able to live more effectively, serve others better, and help establish or maintain high moral and ethical standards in their professions after graduation. They should hear this idea expressed so frequently at the university that it would be an integral part of their thinking in later life.

It would be helpful, of course, if students could hear the same thing in the communities where they would go to practice their professions. If the old-timers, now well established in the community, demonstrated by their actions that they were following acceptable codes of ethics, there was little question, I thought, that their examples would be followed by the newcomers. I realized that this was not likely to be the case, because it is a curious paradox that, while people of all races and nations have discovered independently and preserved in their literature the essence of moral law, they have consistently failed to use moral law in their everyday lives. I realized that this could mean that traits inherent in the human race may make it impossible for people to live together wisely and effectively. If this is true, the defect may prove to be a fatal factor that will lead to racial extinction, just as other groups of organisms have become extinct because they could not adapt to changing conditions on earth. Was it possible that people could not adapt to the power made available by the nuclear revolution of the midtwentieth century? It was a disquieting question.

I became so interested in trying to promote the ethical use of professional competence that I made it the subject of a talk that I gave to many groups during the early 1950s— including the Central States Association of Business Officers, the School of Banking of the University of Wisconsin, the American College of Life Underwriters, and Bell Telephone personnel at a regional meeting in Galveston, Texas. I'll try to find a copy of the talk and send it on to you.

Of course, my efforts were fruitless. According to a survey made by *Look* magazine in 1960 and reported in the issue of March 29 under the title "The Age of Payola," the situation had actually worsened during the preceding decade.

The article reminded its readers that a New York borough president had been indicted on charges of conspiracy to obstruct justice and three violations of the city charter. Meat markets and fuel-oil dealers had been accused of defrauding the public of millions of dollars a year, with the cooperation of city inspectors. In Chicago police officers had been arraigned on charges of conspiring with a confessed burglar.

On the national scene a Mississippi grand jury had refused to indict accused murderers. Charles Van Doren had made $129,000 on a rigged television show, had lied to a grand jury, had said he was sorry, had been praised by congressmen for his frankness—and had kept the money. In Washington, D.C., a most trusted assistant of the president had accepted gifts from Bernard Goldfine, a wealthy industrialist and had made phone calls on his behalf. Many other examples were given.

The author of the *Look* article, William Attwood, reported that the survey group had met with extensive rationalizing while conducting the survey. He said: "Out of the confusion, a new American code of ethics seems to be evolving. Its terms are seldom stated in so many words, but it adds up to this: Whatever you do is all right if it's legal, or if you disapprove of the law. It's all right if it doesn't hurt anybody. And it's all right if it's part of accepted business practice."

Clearly the situation was bad in 1960. I am afraid it is even worse today. Unethical behavior appears to have invaded our universities, particularly in the administration of intercollegiate athletics. Not long ago four universities of the Pacific Coast Conference were given probationary status as a result of various charges ranging from violating recruiting rules through altering transcripts of entering athletes to giving university credit for classes not attended. Several other institutions have faced similar charges in the past, including the University of Oklahoma. One redeeming feature about the Pacific Coast situation was that the violations were discovered by the institutions' academic representatives to the conference and the probationary status was self-imposed.

It appears that when money is involved morality and ethics are pushed to the background. A fund-raising rock-and-roll concert was staged in the OU stadium not long ago, though it is well known that such affairs are often large-scale drug and liquor fests in which sheer numbers effectively prevent law enforcement. Under such circumstances how could the university be effective in meeting its most basic responsibility in future years—that of helping students develop the moral and ethical attitudes that may be necessary for the preservation of our way of life?

A serious cause for pessimism about the higher levels of learning comes to us in *Betrayers of the Truth,* by William Broad and Nicholas Wade (published by Simon and Schuster in 1983). A portion of the book was printed by permission by the TWA *Ambassador* in December, 1982. It described alleged hedging, plagiarism, and fraud by scientific researchers in some of the country's most prestigious institutions. The authors report, discouragingly, that the associates of those accused have been hesitant to give helpful testimony, tending rather to make excuses for those accused.

As you can see, I have described a bleak situation. But

as I told you at the beginning of the letter, I can only spot-light the problem. I wish that I could suggest a remedy.

Affectionately,

P.S. While sorting through my files the other day, I came across a copy of a speech I gave back in 1945 dealing with the use of knowledge. It may be of interest to you [see Appendix 2].

On Ethics and Morality

Dear Bill,

You asked whether I had formed an answer to the second, two-part question in my correspondent's questionnaire: "If you could tell your son only one thing upon graduation from college, what would you tell him? Does your university tell this to the sons of other men?" I did, indeed, come up with an answer, but it took a great deal of time and effort.

Only one thing was obvious as I began my search for an answer. I should try to tell my son something that might be useful to him as he put to use in later life the knowledge he had accumulated as an undergraduate—useful in daily life as well as in the practice of a profession. It should be helpful in his future relations not only with his fellow members of a community but with customers or clients as well. It should have, I thought, moral or ethical implications. It should have the objective of developing proper attitudes for daily living.

But this thought produced a morass of difficult questions. What are ethics and morals? What are proper attitudes? What is moral law? A dictionary was helpful to a degree; it defined "ethics" as "the science of moral duty, or, more broadly, the science of ideal human behavior." It was clear from this definition that "ethics" and "moral law" were approximately equivalent and that both involved ideal human behavior, but the dictionary did not define ideal human behavior. And, after reflecting on my experiences with people through the years, I was quite sure that I had never encountered ideal human behavior, and I suspected that it did not exist. Like other ideal situations, it was probably a much-sought objective—perhaps sometimes approached but never

118

achieved. I had the impression that most people thought of ideal human behavior only in terms of how other people should behave. The dictionary had not been very helpful. Where then could I find a reliable guide to moral law and human behavior—a guide to ethical living concisely stated and generally accepted in a historical sense?

After delving into the matter a bit, including a conversation with a friend in the Philosophy Department, I reached the conclusion that our ideas of ethics and moral law have developed historically as a part of religious thought. I knew little, if anything, about comparative religions, but my philosopher friend referred me to Lewis Browne's *The World's Great Scriptures.* He thought that a careful reading of the work might lead to discovery of a basic principle upon which the world's great religious philosophers had agreed. Such agreement should establish the validity of the principle, and from it all might emerge an answer to the question, "What would I tell my son?" You will wonder, of course, why I should spend so much time on a matter of this kind when so many other pressing problems were demanding my attention. The answer is that I simply could not dismiss the question from my mind. It would intrude into my thoughts with annoying frequency, even when I was engaged in conferences having to do with serious university problems.

So, one afternoon, I went to the university library and checked out Browne's book, the contents of which, at preliminary examination, seemed formidable. I was thoroughly convinced that reading it carefully, searching, perhaps futilely, for agreement among the many scriptures, would be a dreary experience.

I was most pleasantly surprised that evening to find that the author, midway in his preface, had summarized the material I sought. He pointed out that each of the world's great scriptures contained the essence of what Christians call the

Golden Rule. Confucius taught moral law as a part of religion. He said, "Is there one maxim which ought to be acted upon throughout one's whole life? Surely it is a maxim of lovingkindness: do not unto others what you would not have them do unto you." The same basic principle was reported in writings having to do with Brahmanism: "Do not unto others that which would cause you pain if done unto you." Buddhism: "Hurt not others in ways that you yourself would find hurtful." Taoism: "Regard your neighbor's gain as your own gain, and your neighbor's loss as your own loss." Zoroastrianism: "That nature alone is good which refrains from doing unto another whatsoever is not good for itself." Islam: "No one of you is a believer until he desires for his brother that which he desires for himself." Judaism: "What is hateful to you, do not to your fellow men. That is the entire law; all the rest is commentary." Christianity: "All things whatsoever ye would that men should do to you, do ye evenso to them; for this is the law and the prophets."

There, tersely stated, was the principle that had found universal acceptance—one upon which all religious philosophers had agreed. It provided the answer to my question. Certainly, if I could tell my son only one thing, I would tell him, "Do unto others as you would have others do unto you." If he was able to grasp the implications of this statement, he would need no other guide to living, for certainly, as the ancient Jewish writer had put it in the Talmud: "That is the entire law. All the rest is commentary."

Of course, I realized that it would be one thing to hear these words but quite another to make effective use of them in daily living. A practical young man might well ask, "What place do ethics and moral law have in the highly competitive existence that faces those entering the professions today?" Competition, the young man has been told, is traditional in our American way of life. Rugged individualism has made our country strong. How can one observe the Golden Rule and still be practical? Does it mean the elimination of competition, or the desire to get along in the world? Those were good questions that deserved thoughtful answers.

But, I thought, I could assure my son that ethical living and the observance of the Golden Rule need not eliminate competition or the desire to get ahead in the world. The rule only implies that such competition and effort to get ahead will be based entirely on one's ability, efficiency, and willingness to exert honest effort. The purpose of education should be to develop our ability, to increase our efficiency, and to make us see the value of honest effort—but not to enable us to take advantage of others. Under the Golden Rule trickery or subterfuge of any kind in dealing with others would be eliminated. Success would be determined by ability, efficiency, and industry. Success would be measured by the quality of service to associates or clients, and the integrity of relations with those in one's professional world.

Reflecting on these ideas, and discussing them with a few of my young acquaintances, the question arose, "How can we make practical application of the Golden Rule in daily living and be sure that we are actually following it?" Was there a specific test that could be applied in family, community, or business relationships? In most situations, an individual is likely to be at least slightly prejudiced in his own favor and, even with the best of intentions, fail to live up to the spirit of the rule. Then one bright young student produced the answer, suggesting that, in any situation when dealing with another, one should merely imagine that the situation is reversed and then ask the question, "Would I be willing to accept what I am proposing?" If an honest affirmative answer could be given, there would be no need for doubt.

Two or three years after all of this took place, I was

121

invited to deliver the conferment address for the American College of Life Underwriters at a meeting at Washington University, in Saint Louis, Missouri. I was given generous latitude in the choice of a subject, and to help me make the choice, the president of the organization sent me various materials concerning its activities. I found that the American College was a national examining or certifying board that had been organized in 1927 for the purpose of encouraging sound insurance education and the effective use of education in the insurance profession. Each year examinations designed to test the candidate's character and ability to apply his learning were given in more than one hundred institutions scattered throughout the country. Those who passed the examinations were designated "chartered life underwriters." I was to address a group of successful candidates at Washington University.

Glancing through the materials I had received, I noticed with great interest that the American College had incorporated the Golden Rule as a requirement for the designation "chartered life underwriter." Each recipient was required to affirm as follows: "I shall in the light of all the circumstances surrounding my client, which I shall make every conscientious effort to ascertain and to understand, give him that service which, had I been in the same circumstances, I would have applied to myself." I was so heartened by this discovery that I decided to use "The Ethical Use of Professional Competence" as the subject for my Saint Louis talk. In the speech I suggested that a slight modification of that splendid charge to the Chartered Life Underwriters would be useful in the nonprofessional lives of all citizens: "I shall in the light of all the circumstances surrounding my neighbor or my associate, which I shall make every consciencious effort to ascertain and to understand, give him that treatment and consideration which, had I been in the same circumstances, I would have applied to myself."

It seemed to me that it would be very difficult to devise a charge more basically sound, more conducive to good attitudes and values, or more in keeping with the wisdom that is our heritage from past ages. I thought that it should be basic in the education of all people.

So, you see, I did find an answer to the question, "What would I tell my son?" The answer to the second part of the question, "Is your university telling this to other men's sons?" would have had to be in the negative. There is little evidence in the professional world that young people are receiving the message from any source, and society suffers as a consequence.

In case you are curious, I did not fill out the questionnaire.

Affectionately,

P.S. In my last letter, I mentioned that I would try to find and send you a copy of one of the talks I gave on the ethical use of professional competence. I am enclosing one that I gave in 1956 to the School of Banking at the University of Wisconsin [see Appendix 3]. As you will see, the idea for the talk came from the man's questionnaire.

When the President Is Away from the Campus

February 25

Dear Bill,

It was amusing to read your account of the happenings at your school while you were on a speaking tour—visiting alumni groups in Washington and other eastern cities. Theory has it that one measure of a well-managed institution is that the head man can be gone for an appreciable period of time, a month or so, without being missed by the general public. He has things so well organized that his administration runs on its own momentum. On the other hand, if this is true for a prolonged absence, it may mean that he is not really needed. I was always careful not to test the latter possibility by being away from the University of Oklahoma for more than two or three weeks at a time until I had announced my retirement, effective June 30, 1968.

Your letter reminded me of the 1966-67 school year at OU. The events of the fall that year were pleasant and reassuring. Student unrest seemed at a minimum; there were occasional minor grumblings but no demonstrations or confrontations. The football team defeated both Texas and Nebraska, thus at least partly negating a loss to Oklahoma State University and putting to rest any worry that fans would press for a new coach. There had been no drug incidents of any kind on the campus, and no detected—or at least no publicized—"immorality." The OU College Bowl team (remember those interesting instant-recall television contests?) had retired undefeated and, though I did not know it at the time, would later win the national championship.

124

One of our seniors had been successful in his competition for a Rhodes Scholarship, and I basked happily in the thought that OU was third among state universities in the production of Rhodes scholars and ninth among all institutions, including such prestigious places as Yale, Harvard, and MIT.

Of course, there had been a little money missing from a bookstore account, but that did not seem serious at the time. It could well be a bookkeeping error of some kind.

The preholiday season had been so peaceful that it seemed a good time for Cleo and me to take a month's vacation jaunt to the South Pacific Islands. At our age, we reflected, one must get some traveling done before it is too late. We flew to Tahiti on December 30 and then took a boat to Moorea, an island in French Polynesia, where we had reservations for a few days at a seaside hotel. During our visit there it occurred to me that it might already be too late for us to take that kind of junket. The damsels who flitted about the beach and hotel grounds were definitely of a different generation.

But the news from home that we received sporadically during early January seemed to justify our decision to take the trip. A letter from our son, received at Christchurch, New Zealand, contained the happy news that our wrestling team had defeated the team from Oklahoma State University and that our basketball team had won over Nebraska, supposedly a powerhouse in the Big Eight. Fortunately, we did not receive any other reports concerning university activities while we were traveling.

When we arrived home on February 1, after flying without sleep from Honolulu to Oklahoma City, I anticipated a short nap before reporting to my office. After all, an hour or so, after an absence of a month, shouldn't make any difference.

But as I was making my way wearily up the front stairs

125

of the president's house with a piece of rather heavy luggage in each hand, thinking of the bed waiting on the second floor, the front-door bell rang. Cleo, who had glanced out the living-room window, reported that the county sheriff's car was in the driveway. Leaving the luggage at the top landing of the stairs, I returned to the first floor to find out what bad news awaited me at the front door. The sheriff was there with the question, Could I provide a picture of the "missing bursar"? Not knowing that we had lost a bursar, I was understandably perplexed, but I said that I had no pictures of anyone associated with the bursar's office, and soon the sheriff's car pulled out of our driveway. I gave up the idea of a nap and went to my office, where, in a short time, I learned a great many things.

While I was gone, additional money had been reported missing from the bookstore account. The assistant bursar could not be found, and sleuth-minded reporters had related the missing money to his disappearance. Our public-information office had been accused of withholding information that would have made it possible to prove this.

The missing bursar was only one of several matters which, at first thought seemed to require attention. During a relatively mild altercation in the Union Building, a foreign student had pushed or shoved a member of the Students for a Democratic Society, and the incident had been reported in the newspapers as a near riot. The news stories contained hints that matters might be getting out of control at the state university.

A woman student had been apprehended with a small amount of marijuana in her possession. She reported that she had obtained the drug from a graduate student who was teaching part time in the Department of English and was thus technically a member of the university faculty. Was the faculty contributing to the delinquency of students at the state university?

Somewhat in support of this possibility, I found several letters on my desk concerning the scheduled appearance on our campus of two well-publicized theologians during our annual Conference on Religion. Thomas J. J. Altizer, of "God is dead" fame, and James A. Pike, who contended that Jesus was not *the* Son of God but only *a* son of God, had seemed likely choices by the students who had planned the conference. The letters contained hints that these theologians should not be permitted to appear at the university.

Also on my desk was a copy of a memorandum that had been sent to the regents of the University, the regents for higher education, members of the state legislature, and the governor of Oklahoma. The memorandum charged that the School of Art had been using nude models in its art classes. The subject, sternly stated near the top of the first page, was "the horrible practice of hiring college girls to strip stark naked and expose their breasts and sex organs before groups of men." The writer said that he had explored the situation thoroughly with the dean of the College of Fine Arts, and he had used three legal-sized pages, typed single-spaced, to report his findings. Near the end of the memorandum was a recommendation that everyone who had been involved in permitting nude models to be used in the art classes should be dismissed from the university, including the president.

Ordinarily, I would not have been concerned about the charge that we used nude models in our art classes at OU. The problem had come to the surface, without serious consequence, at approximately five-year intervals since I had become president back in 1944. But the details in the memorandum, which suggested that the university was depraving young women and perhaps condemning them to lives of pros-

127

titution, widely distributed to groups capable of making trouble for the university, gave me pause. I remembered, with satisfaction, that I had announced my retirement at the beginning of the school year—thus giving the regents two years to find my successor.

I reflected that I might have done better to skip the South Seas trip and stay at home. Of course, everything that happened would have happened regardless of my presence or absence, but I would have become aware of the happenings one at a time, instead of having them all thrust upon me at once. I decided that I could not recommend university administration as a profession, but, on the other hand, I concluded that there may not be any completely satisfactory way to make a living.

As I left the office about six that evening, I resolved firmly to keep University affairs out of my mind until the next day—not take my problems home with me. But this was not to be. At the dinner table, Braden, who thought that I should be brought up to date on matters he considered important, reported that the basketball team had lost practically all of its games played during January, and there were rumors that the coach planned to resign. By way of supplement to this unhappy report, he told me that the wrestling team, which we had hoped might win a national championship that year, had been defeated by Michigan State the week before.

When I suggested that we discontinue discussion of University matters, the lad turned to matters of domestic concern. The parakeet had escaped from its cage and had been missing for several days. The mystery had been partly solved when wing and tail feathers were found in the guest bathroom on the first floor. Our pet Siamese cat, Sigal, was a strong suspect in the case, but positive proof was lacking. No feathers had been found around his mouth, and he had maintained an air of innocence. When I asked, with scarcely concealed petulance, whether anything had gone well during our absence, Braden replied cheerfully that "Mother's house plants are in good condition."

After this rather dismal first day at home, things looked much better the next morning. I found that a vice-president had arranged for an independent audit of the bookstore operations, with the promise that the results would be made available to the public. The Office of Media Information had countered the adverse newspaper publicity with carefully prepared news releases. The dean of the College of Fine Arts had successfully interpreted to the president of the Board of Regents the use of nude models in our art classes, and the president had been reasonably successful in quieting criticism from politicians and the public. The only unsolved problem seemed to be the coming appearance of Altizer and Pike on the campus—a matter that I thought could be handled without serious consequences.

The manner in which my administrative associates had handled their delegated responsibilities during my absence pleased me very much. It was clear that, as I approached my final year as president of OU, I had developed an organization that could function effectively during my absence. I had always believed that specific and complete delegation of authority and responsibility was the sine qua non of good university administration.

I should emphasize, however, that unspecific and partial delegation will not be effective. If members of the president's staff do not understand clearly the limits of their authority and responsibility, and if they therefore feel that they must consult with him before making final decisions, they are likely to use the president as a psychological crutch, thus restricting the development of their potential. Psychological strength, like physical strength, cannot be achieved until all the crutches are discarded and the individuals learn to walk — and think — without their aid.

Perhaps the relatively minor unsolved problems that have accumulated in your office during your brief absence wound up there because you had not been specific and complete in delegating authority and responsibility to the members of your staff. You might give this possibility some thought, especially in view of the fact that, as time goes on, the number of hours that you can give to campus affairs will diminish — necessarily so because of the increasing time you will have to give to fund-raising and other activities as you represent your institution off campus.

Affectionately,

The Case of the Missing Bursar

Dear Bill,

You ask why an assistant bursar was thought responsible for the embezzlement of money from the bookstore. Your question reminded me of the saddest, most sordid, and most thoroughly unpleasant series of incidents in my tenure as president. An account of what happened may help you maintain perspective sometime in the future when almost unbelievable events occur within your university family.

When the sheriff came to see me only a few minutes after I had returned from the South Seas excursion and asked for a picture of the missing bursar, I was greatly concerned. The University bursar, John Freeman, was a thoroughly upright public servant and close personal friend of mine (he was also the husband of one of the best secretaries—Panthea May Evans—I have ever had). When I found that the missing person was an *assistant* bursar, I was relieved, though rapidly accumulating information made my relief short-lived.

You are right in assuming that the money must have been taken by someone who worked in the bookstore. Among the employees at the book exchange that summer was a young woman whom I shall call Kate Brown. Following an unsuccessful first marriage, which she ended with a small daughter to support, Kate had enrolled at the university to work for a degree in accounting. She was handicapped by a total loss of hearing, but she read lips so skillfully that the average person was not aware of her handicap. She made a very good record as a student, and, when she graduated, Jim Mayfield, the compassionate manager of the bookstore, gave her a job. She performed so well that over a period of months she be-

131

came informally regarded as accountant for the store—completely trusted by the management and her associates. There were never shortages or other problems with the store's accounts, and Mayfield relied on her increasingly as time went on.

On at least one occasion Kate had been seen having dinner with a man whom I shall call Jim Boyles, who was employed by the university as an assistant bursar. During the fall of 1966, however, she married another member of the university's auditing staff. Her husband turned out to be an unsatisfactory employee and was dismissed from the university in December, only a few weeks after the marriage.

The unemployed husband caused immediate and serious problems for Kate. He asked her to give him money from the book exchange account, and, when she refused, she immediately became a battered wife—badly abused by what appeared to be a sadistic husband. Unable to withstand such mistreatment, she finally gave in and took money.

Late in December, Kate was hospitalized and while she was absent from work, it was discovered that $2,300 was missing from the bookstore's accounts (this was the missing money I mentioned in my last letter). I had learned about it from Bill Jordan, the University's internal auditor, only a few days before we left on the South Pacific trip.

After we left, word of the missing money reached the news media, and reporters were quickly on the scene. University personnel were reluctant to tell the whole story of what had happened. That is understandable, because Kate was a well-liked, trusted employee, and no one wanted to give a statement that might damage her reputation until University auditors had determined exactly what had happened. But the reticence of Mayfield and others only stimulated the curiosity of reporters, and several speculative stories appeared in the papers.

The situation was to be confused by further developments. On January 16, 1967, Jim Boyles (the assistant bursar mentioned earlier), called in to report that he was not feeling well and would not be in the office that day. He said that he was calling from a doctor's office in Norman, but the call was later traced to Tecumseh, a few miles east of Norman. Jim was never seen again in Norman. He was reported as a missing person, and a week later his parents were on the scene trying to help find him.

In the meantime, innovative reporters had found a picture of Boyles taken at the reception following Kate's second marriage. It was recalled that Jim had taken Kate to dinner on at least one occasion before her marriage. From this it was reasoned that surely there must be some connection between the missing money and the missing assistant bursar. Reporters pressed for information concerning possible additional inroads that might have been made into university finances. The outside audit mentioned in my last letter turned up an additional shortage of $1,074.15 in the bookstore account, but there were no other shortages.

The disappearance of the assistant bursar continued to be a mystery. An examination of his apartment in the Student Union Building indicated that he had not taken any clothing or other personal items with him when he vanished. An account in one of the local banks remained unused. Missing only were the articles he had with him that day and the red Mustang that he drove. All of this suggested foul play of some kind.

Early in March the body of a man was discovered in a desolate area near the Rio Grande just north of the Mexican border east of Brownsville, Texas. The body could not be identified, and the cause of death could not be determined. Justice of the Peace Johnny Gabito, who took part in the investigation, agreed finally—though reluctantly he said—

that the body should be buried with the notation "death from unknown causes" rather than from "natural causes."

For some undisclosed reason Oklahoma police officers working on the assistant bursar's disappearance were led to the Texas area. Pictures of Jim and his red Mustang, along with stories concerning his disappearance, were run in Texas newspapers and during television newscasts. The publicity came to the attention of Thomas Robert Peale, of Browns-ville, who thought he recognized the red Mustang pictured in the newscast. He convincingly described identifying marks on the vehicle and said that he had ridden in it, with another man, from Brownsville to San Diego. The trip had been made not long after the body had been discovered in Brownsville. All of this led investigators to suspect that the unidentified person recently buried at Brownsville might be Jim Boyles. An order to exhume the body for a second autopsy was obtained, and a belt buckle with the correct initial was noted. In addition, a high-school class ring with Boyles's initials and the correct date of graduation was found on a finger. Later dental evidence proved conclusively that the missing bursar had been found.

The red Mustang and the victim's credit cards were used by someone for a long time, with charges ranging from California into Canada. The automobile was finally discovered in a used-car lot, but apparently had changed hands two or three times. The whereabouts of the missing bursar had been determined, but the events leading to his disappearance remained a mystery.

Kate, after leaving the hospital, was tried and convicted of embezzlement, but because she was able to make restitution of the missing funds, she was given a suspended sentence. All who knew her were convinced that she had taken the money because of pressure from a husband who had serious financial—and emotional—problems.

134

These two tragedies, unrelated except through newspaper speculation, produced a somber atmosphere at the university for several months. It seemed that there would be no end to the discussions over coffee in the Union Building. There were so many unanswered questions concerning Boyles. Was he under someone's influence, or even under duress, when he called from Tecumseh to say that he would not be in his office that day? Was he later killed in Oklahoma and his body transferred to Texas for disposal, or was he killed in Brownsville as a result of quarrels that may have developed as he and another, or others, traveled south?

I know only that I spent countless hours on the sordid problems—problems in no way related to higher education—dealing with reporters, interpreting events to the regents and others, and trying to console the missing man's parents. It was all a part of the job, however, and a president must always be prepared to deal with whatever develops.

Affectionately,

Commencements

Dear Bill,

I agree that your commencement ceremonies probably need overhauling, but I am hard put to suggest anything that might be useful. I am well aware that a graduating class of two thousand or more, with a wide variety of concerns, poses a difficult problem. The traditional ceremony is no longer likely to be appropriate.

Commencement marks the end of a period of formal education during which a group of students have made periodic deposits (credit hours) to a sort of academic bank account kept in the registrar's office. When each student accumulates a sufficient number of credits in his account, he is in a position to make academic payment for a degree and have this fact publicized on graduation day. His name is listed in the commencement program, his degree is formally conferred by the president, and he may walk across the speaker's platform and receive a diploma or something symbolizing a diploma. He may or may not have received an education while accumulating his academic bank account, because comprehensive examinations designed to test total intellectual accomplishment unfortunately are not customarily given as a prerequisite to graduation. Piecemeal achievements are regarded as sufficient evidence of overall achievement.

Of course, the word "commencement" connotes more than past achievement. It implies the beginning of something. When used in connection with graduation ceremonies, I suppose it means that the graduating class is now in a position to face the world—to cope with the multitude of social, economic, political, and emotional problems in the social structure beyond the campus.

At the time I became president of OU, we were using the conventional plan for commencement—processional, music, preliminary remarks with introduction of guests, commencement address, conferring of degrees, calling of names of graduates as they marched across the speaker's platform to receive their degrees. This worked fairly well with the smaller graduating classes we had at that time.

After the end of World War II, however, with the dramatic increse in enrollment followed by much larger graduating groups, the commencement committee decided that bachelor's-degree candidates would no longer cross the stage and have their names called. Candidates for higher degrees, including law and medicine, were presented diplomas individually and were hooded by the president. This change, of course, disturbed many parents, who attended commencement expecting to see their progeny recognized individually.

As time went on and graduating groups continued to grow, we had to move the commencement program to the stadium because no other facility on the campus was large enough to accommodate the graduates with their relatives and friends—who sometimes numbered as many as twenty thousand. With this change came another. Because of the increase in the number of master's degree candidates the commencement committee decided that only the doctoral candidates would walk across the stage, have their names called and be hooded.

Outdoor commencements can be a great success if the weather is good. But Oklahoma weather, especially in springtime, is unpredictable. As Will Rogers said about the climate of his home state, "If you don't like the weather, wait a minute; it will likely change." Fickle weather caused us em-

barrassment on one or two occasions when we invited distinguished speakers to appear on our commencement program
only to have a rainstorm force cancellation of the ceremonies.
In addition to the embarrassment there was a financial loss;
the speaker's honorarium had to be paid whether or not he
spoke.

All of this led to speculation concerning the need for a
commencement speaker. Was it really necessary to have a
thirty- or forty-minute talk preliminary to an already long
ceremony?

It was suspected that university presidents generally favored the traditional commencement address. It provided an
opportunity for reciprocal courtesies involving significant
financial benefits—honoraria. A president who invited the
head of an institution to give his school's commencement
address could reasonably expect an invitation to appear at his
friend's institution on a similar occasion at some later date.
Politically oriented presidents could make significant head-
way by inviting prominent political figures to their campuses.
The practice could be useful also in fund raising; heads of
corporations, and others who possessed or controlled wealth
almost certainly could be wooed effectively through an invitation to give a commencement address. Then, too, one should
not dismiss the possibility that the commencement speaker
might say something really worthwhile—something that
would be remembered with benefit by the graduating group.
But even with careful thought, I could not remember an example of such.

Most of the student members of the commencement
committee agreed that neither those who receive degrees
nor the parents and friends assembled to witness the occasion were likely to be much interested in a commencement
address. It was suggested that few, if any, came because of

the speaker, and it was even possible that some resented the time they spent listening to the speech.

As I listened to this discussion, I was reminded of a commencement talk that I had given at Okmulgee High School two years before. The ceremonies were to be conducted in the stadium, and it was arranged that I would meet the superintendent there half an hour before they were to begin.

When I arrived for the occasion, I found that the seats of the stadium were built into the side of a hill that sloped downward to the football field below. I stood for a few minutes at the top of the stadium awaiting the arrival of the superintendent. I looked down at the assembling crowd, the speaker's stand, and the seats for graduates on the football field, beyond a beautiful field of green alfalfa to a stream that flowed lazily with splendid oak trees on each bank. The sun was beginning to set, and a very gentle breeze indicated that a beautiful evening was in prospect.

I said to a gentleman standing on my right: "What a beautiful evening we have. It should be a most pleasant commencement ceremony."

He replied: "Yes, we do have a fine evening, and a fine graduating class. It could be a very nice affair if old Cross isn't too long-winded tonight." It occurred to me that the man's remark probably summarized very well the public's attitude toward commencement speakers.

As I drove home later that evening, I gave the matter serious thought. Although I had heard a goodly number of commencement talks, I could not remember a single one that really seemed to fit the occasion. I decided that the most useful statement I had heard at a commencement ceremony was made during the concluding remarks of the superintendent of the Ponca City, Oklahoma, High School.

The superintendent in question had held office for several years. One spring during the late 1940s he invited me to give his school's commencement address. After I had given my best effort for that evening and the diplomas had been handed out, the superintendent gave his charge to the graduating class. At the conclusion of his remarks he said that the best advice he could give was contained in a story. He said that some crows were flying aimlessly above a California highway one day when, to their delight, a huge truckload of prunes was suddenly wrecked below, scattering prunes on the side of the road and into an adjacent field. The crows descended and gorged themselves on the delicious fruit. Most of the birds then departed, but there were five who had overeaten and were unable to become airborne. The five crows climbed on the handle of a rake a farmer had left leaning against the fence and spent the night there in the shelter of an oak tree that grew in the corner of the field.

The next morning one of the birds flew off the handle and headed north, only to fly a few feet and then fall to the earth dead. A second took off headed east and soon plummeted to the ground. A third headed south, only to meet a similar fate, and the fourth flew west from the handle and crashed headlong into a bush. The fifth bird remained on the handle wondering about it all. A wise old owl high in the oak tree was heard to remark, "Well, that certainly proves the point." The fifth crow looked up into the tree and asked, "What point does it prove?" The owl replied, "Never fly off the handle when you're full of prunes."

At the next meeting of the commencement committee I agreed that we would not have a commencement speaker in the future but would make commencement a family affair with emphasis on what the graduates had accomplished at the University.

For the next fifteen years or so, the OU commencement

program did not list a speaker. The new plan seemed to work very well and attracted enough people to fill the north end of the stadium. More attention was given to introductions of groups in the audience, who were invited to stand and be recognized—parents of the graduates, grandparents of the graduates, children of the graduates, graduates who had served with the armed forces, graduates who expected to serve with the armed forces, and so on.

After the degrees were conferred, I spent some time delivering a charge to the recipients. One favorite theme that I used was to challenge the graduates to be as aggressively critical in community, state, and national affairs as they had been critical of the University during their undergraduate days.

On each of these occasions, I always experienced a tinge of regret that not all recipients of degrees could be brought across the stage and have their names called. The candidates from the various colleges were recognized only when their dean invited them to stand and receive applause when their degrees were conferred.

Since my retirement from the presidency, the university has staged a ceremony that represents a compromise between the conventional procedure and the plan I followed. Commencement is now held in the recently constructed Lloyd Noble Center, which accommodates about thirteen thousand people.

In addition to the speaker's stand, where the president presides and confers the degrees, four additional stations with platforms are provided on the floor of the center. After the degrees are conferred, the candidates from each college march across one of the platforms, where a symbolic scroll is presented by the dean. The scroll consists of a picture of some portion of the university and is suitable for framing. The diplomas are mailed to the graduates a few weeks later.

141

All of this is somewhat confusing, because the graduates are streaming across four platforms at the same time, and no names are called. However, alert parents and friends are usually able to spot their students during the handshake and presentation of the scroll.

I should add also that the university is again using a commencement speaker, invariably an individual of prominence in the political or financial world. Everything is accomplished in less than two hours. Perhaps that plan would work for you.

Affectionately,

P.S.: Later I recalled an article that appeared in the February, 1952, issue of the *Journal of Higher Education.* It was written by Garff B. Wilson, chairman of the Committee on Public Ceremonies in the University of California, Berkeley. Wilson, aware of problems in commencement ceremonies for large graduating classes, visited Yale, Harvard, Columbia, Cornell, and MIT to see how these institutions handled their commencements. His article, "Commencement at the Large Universities," reports his findings. You may find helpful suggestions in it.

Population Problems

Dear Bill,

One statement in your last letter was of special interest to me—the difficulty of projecting future population pressures in the different regions of the country and the impact these pressures will have on student enrollments in our colleges and universities. Reliable projections of this kind could be extremely useful in planning future campus development. About all we can safely say is that world population will continue to increase and that our own country will be involved in the increase.

I should add that, to me, the increase in world population is the most impressive and ominous of modern problems. I am especially concerned about what has taken place during the twentieth century. It took from the beginning of mankind until 1830 to reach a world population of one billion, but it took only one hundred years to reach the second billion and only thirty years to reach the third billion in 1960. Today, by a conservative estimate, there are four billion of us on the earth's surface. Thus, in one generation, as many people have been added to the world's population as in all previous history. And the end is not in sight.

Of course, the most spectacular increases have occurred in the countries of the Eastern Hemisphere—especially the Orient. But the increase in our own country, and the impact that it has had on our environment is disturbing to me.

Unfortunately, our economic system is based on the expectancy of increasing population. Business and industry have come to be based on an exponential increase in demand for goods and services. Advertising is designed to persuade

143

people to want things they haven't wanted and to buy things they don't need with money they don't have. The people have been receptive to these persuasive efforts. As a result, our economy during the last several decades, with only occasional setbacks, has developed at an exponential rate that cannot be maintained indefinitely. With an expanding population, combined with an amazing series of technological developments and what seemed to be an unlimited supply of cheap energy, we have enjoyed an economic growth and a standard of living that our descendants surely will regard with something akin to disbelief.

Because, contrary to what our industrialists and politicians seem to believe, growth in numbers on our planet is finite. While energy problems may be solved, natural resources and available space limit growth to a level as yet not determined. But the time surely will come—and it may have arrived for higher education—when we will need to cope with a no-growth situation. Plateaus will finally be reached, and thereafter improved standards of living or the continuance of those we now enjoy will depend on our ability to control populations and refine our industrial and business operations. While at least some individuals of the business world must be aware of this, their awareness is not detectable. Greed for wealth in their time dominates their thinking, and the result has been and is a shameless exploitation of natural resources that, used wisely, could maintain a reasonable world population indefinitely.

Mary Eleanor Clark, a member of the faculty of San Diego State University, summarized the situation well in an interview in 1981 with an editor of *U.S. News and World Report.* Professor Clark said in part:

> We're rushing along with technology and the dangers we are creating are making our path to the future narrower and

narrower and the cliff edges on each side of it steeper and steeper. We are rushing "up there" toward our ultimate goal — the infinite technology — hoping that we're not going to fall off along the way.

In just a few decades, we have used up half the world's fossil-fuel supplies, which took millions of years to be created. We are rapidly depleting the ground water that was deposited during the Ice Age. Topsoil is draining out of the Mississippi River at a rate of 15 tons per second. None of these resources will ever be replaced. One of the lessons biology teaches is that no population can long exceed the carrying capacity of its environment without a crash.

The entire report of the interview would be well worth your reading. I'll look it up and send it to you.

There is biological evidence that exponential growth of any kind always leads to disaster. For example, a colony of organisms growing on a cultural medium in a bacteriological laboratory will reproduce abundantly as long as they are able to dispose of their metabolites — the by-products or wastes of their living processes. But when the organisms reach such numbers that they are no longer able to dispose of the wastes, the colony dies. The same thing happens in nature. A small number of staphylococci can grow vigorously on a human forearm and cause a boil or carbuncle. Things go well with the organisms for a time, but finally, with exponential increase in number, the colony self-destructs through the accumulation of excessive metabolites. Before this happens in nature, however, a few organisms move on from the old environment to a new one. As the carbuncle or boil matures and finally breaks on a human forearm, another may appear on the same forearm or elsewhere.

Some thoughtful biologists and sociologists, reflecting on world population pressures and the resulting environmental destruction, have become inclined to regard the human

145

race as the causal agent of a kind of planetary disease, in much the sense that staphylococci are the causal agents of skin diseases. Symptoms of world infection are the great scars on its surface caused by industrial development and the mismanagement of forested areas. Other symptoms include the extreme pollution of the planet's water and air through the careless disposal of the waste of civilization. Polluted urban areas such as Los Angeles, Denver, Phoenix, and New York, on the earth's skin have been likened to the boils and carbuncles caused by bacteria on human skin.

With a continuing increase in population, it has been pointed out, we can expect an increase in the manifestation and severity of these symptoms of planetary sickness until our planet becomes so sick that it can no longer provide a suitable environment for human beings and perhaps many other higher organisms.

One of my pessimistic friends once suggested that our efforts to achieve interplanetary travel could at best only spread the human disease a little more widely in the universe.

Reflection on all of this the other evening caused a small discussion group of which I was a member to consider the possibility that the human race will turn out to be a biological disaster, causing havoc not only to its own members but to other organisms as well. Probably nonhuman inhabitants of the planet would agree that this is possible. Human exploitation and mistreatment of lesser evolved neighbors have been scarcely short of shameful, with little or no recognition of the rights of other species. I thought of this the other evening while watching horses being mistreated in a John Wayne movie, and on another occasion when I read about a season for deer hunting with bows and arrows; and I was depressed some time ago when I read of a plan to build a jet landing strip on the bottom of the Ngorongoro crater in

Africa so that human beings could have an easy means of viewing the magnificent animal life there.

Glancing back over the preceding paragraphs, it appears that I may have wandered a bit from the original issue. I suspect, however, that this is not an uncommon trait among those who are living in their fourth quarter of a century. What I have said also could be interpreted as extreme pessimism. While pessimism may be another trait of those suffering from excessive maturation, I really did not mean it to be so in this letter.

As I see it, the human race must solve two problems if it is to continue to survive: control of population and conservation of the planet's resources. While we have made very little progress toward the solution of either problem, I do not consider the situation hopeless. Because the potential for solution exists in higher education, it is only necessary to develop that potential. I believe that it was H. G. Wells who once spoke of the race between "education and disaster." It is the responsibility of the world's universities to see that the race is not lost.

Affectionately,

Retirement

Dear Bill,

I, too, enjoyed reading *The Sooner Story: Ninety Years at the University of Oklahoma, 1890-1980* [Norman: University of Oklahoma Foundation, 1980]. It is a very good capsule account of what has happened since OU opened its doors back in the days before statehood. My contributions as president are exaggerated, but, of course, I enjoyed it.

Yes, my tenure as president was long—nearly a quarter of a century—though it did not set a record for state universities. I was, however, impressed by the thought that when I retired I had been president of OU for nearly one-third of the time that the school had been in existence.

At meetings of the Association of State University Presidents during my final years there would be occasional speculation about why certain presidents seemed to last almost indefinitely, while the average tenure for the profession was scarcely longer than that of head football coaches—about four years. Many explanations were offered, one of which gave me pause. It was suggested that lengthy tenure of a university president might be related to inadequate performance of his duties. If he had done his job properly, so the theory went, enough people would have been antagonized to cause him to lose his job within a reasonable span of time—perhaps five years.

This idea was corroborated to some extent one evening back in the early sixties, when some state-university presidents were exploring longevity in the job with Harold Willis Dodd, president emeritus of Princeton University. The informal session took place in the afternoon before Dodd was scheduled to give an address at the annual dinner of the Association of American Universities. When he was asked why he thought certain presidents survived and others dropped quickly by the wayside, he stated that in his opinion only two traits were necessary to ensure success in the treacherous profession. The first, he said, is a few gray hairs to give the president a look of distinction when he represents his institution beyond the campus. The second, he said, is an at least mild case of hemorrhoids to give him a look of concern when a problem is brought to his office.

Needless to say, I used Dodd's comment on many occasions in speeches during my retirement year—always with proper acknowledgment, of course.

In response to your question, "Why, after surviving in the job for so long, and apparently in good health, did you decide to leave the job five years before mandatory retirement?" I can best answer with an anecdote.

There was once a young lady of negotiable virtue who did so well in her profession that she was finally able to purchase the establishment in which she worked. Her name was Celeste.

Celeste took over active management of her "house" and operated from a nice desk in an office near the entrance.

A middle-aged man who occasionally patronized the house got into the habit of going into her office to visit—discuss politics, philosophy, or what have you. Celeste was intelligent, and the man enjoyed these conversations very much.

On one occasion when he came in for the usual chat, Celeste was not at her desk or in her office. He proceeded on to what might be called the lineup room, where, to his amazement, he saw Celeste with the rest of the girls, apparently ready for the business of the evening. He walked over to her and said: "Celeste, what in the world has happened?

You shouldn't be here. You own this place. You should be in your office managing it." To this Celeste replied: "I know I shouldn't be here. I know I own the place, and I know that I should be in the front office managing it. But sometimes I get *so* damn fed up with administration."

Like Celeste, I was "fed up with administration." The student confrontations of the sixties, which started on the West Coast and spread across the country, suggested to me that the job of administering a state university might become a bit strenuous for a man of my years. While we had had no trouble at OU, I thought that it was time for a younger man to take over.

I was strengthened in arriving at this decision by the thought that if I remained in the presidency until mandatory retirement I could look forward only to settling in a rocking chair somewhere, hoping for enough energy to rock while I reflected on the aging process. It seemed wise to make a change while I was still young enough to do other things — perhaps become involved in something in which there would be no mandatory retirement.

For eleven years before my retirement from the University I had been a member of the Board of Directors of the Federal Home Loan Bank of Topeka, and for nine of those years I had been chairman of that board. The directors of the bank, which served a four-state area, consisted largely of personnel from the savings-and-loan industry. However, each of the four states was represented by a public-interest director, charged with the responsibility of watchdogging the savings-and-loan industry. I was the public-interest director from Oklahoma.

During my service with the board, I became increasingly interested in thrift institutions — both savings-and-loan institutions and commercial banks. I gave rather thoughtful attention to the impact their activities made on the economic, social, and cultural development of the areas they served. I was impressed mainly by what I thought they should be doing but weren't. I finally decided to retire early from the OU presidency and go into the commercial banking business with the thought that I might be able to make at least minor improvements in the local situation. Four years before my retirement from the OU presidency, I helped organize two new banks, one in Norman and one in Oklahoma City. While I have now been involved for more than twelve years, I must confess that I have not been able to improve the banking industry to any detectable extent.

Banking has been a part-time career, of course. As you know, since my retirement I've also done a good bit of writing about the University and its achievements. With these varied activities, on the whole my postretirement years have been rewarding ones.

You will remember that J. Herbert Hollomon was appointed president designate by the regents to serve during the final year of my presidency. He was given the responsibility of studying the audits operations very closely and developing plans for the future of the University. During that year I was frequently asked whether I was doing a good job tutoring my successor for his new responsibilities. The question reminded me of President Oliver Wilham's reply at Oklahoma State University when he was asked a similar question concerning his successor, President-elect Robert Kamm.

Dr. Wilham replied that he wasn't sure that it was possible for one to tutor his successor in such a situation. Then he told a story about an elderly minister who had announced his retirement. The young minister chosen to succeed him was sent to the church a few months ahead of time so that he could have an opportunity to observe his predecessor in action.

After several weeks of working together, during which

the young minister listened carefully to the older man's sermons each Sunday morning, he asked his friend how he managed to maintain his energy and enthusiasm at such a high level during the fairly long sermons that he preached weekly. The older minister replied: "I keep a glass of what appears to be ice water to the side of the pulpit. It's really vodka on ice, but my congregation doesn't know that. When I feel my enthusiasm waning to any appreciable extent, I take a sip from the glass. I have found this to be very helpful."

Finally it came time for the young minister to preach his first sermon. On a table beside the pulpit was a glass filled with a colorless liquid, from which he sipped frequently.

After the sermon, he asked his predecessor for an opinion of his first effort. The older man replied: "Well, I would say that your energy and enthusiasm were excellent, but there are a few matters of fact that I should bring to your attention. There were ten commandments, not eleven. There were twelve disciples, not ten. But above all you should remember that David merely slew Goliath—he didn't beat the hell out of him."

Now that I have become involved with anecdotes, I find it difficult to stop. I must tell you one more.

During the final months of my retirement year I was asked on several occasions what I planned to do after retirement. Did I expect to serve the institution as a consultant? In response I frequently told a story related by a dean of students during a conference at the University several years ago.

Apparently the dean didn't have a very high regard for consulting services. He told of a tomcat who lived in the neighborhood whose elderly residents tried to maintain as much peace and quiet as possible. The cat caused a problem during his nightly activities, meowing and yowling. The residents of the area finally became sufficiently annoyed that they called on the owner of the cat and urged him to take the animal to a veterinarian for remedial surgery. The owner finally agreed.

After surgery and a short stay in the hospital, the cat returned home. The neighbors, who had become accustomed to quiet while he was away, were startled to hear the same yowling and screeching they had heard before. At first they were not seriously concerned, supposing that it might take a few days for the cat's hormones to diminish to the proper concentration after the removal of their sources. However, after a week had gone by, with no relief, the neighbors decided to call the veterinary and ask for an explanation. The veterinary was very much surprised to hear that there was still a problem. He reported that he had given the cat the best, most complete surgical attention he could provide. He was quite sure that the operation had been a success. He did not understand why the cat still yowled. Then he added, hopefully, "Perhaps now that he is no longer capable of assuming complete responsibility for the situation, he may be acting as a consultant in the neighborhood."

Every inquiry I received reminded me of this story. I always assured my questioner that I had no intention of offering consulting services of any kind after retirement.

I'll end my letter with the above. I have a feeling that I probably should have ended earlier.

Affectionately,

On General Versus Special Education

April 14

Dear Bill,

I surely agree that recent graduates of our colleges and universities seem not to be as well rounded as their predecessors of the century's middle decades. This, I think, is generally conceded by educators throughout the country. Doubtless it is an effect of the turn from general to special education that occurred in the early 1970s. You will remember the trend of those years—the student demands for "relevance" in course offerings and the elimination of required courses for which immediate use in living could not be seen. Of course, those making the demands had scant realization of what is really relevant in preparing for effective living.

The problem you mention was recognized by the National Association of State Universities and Land Grant Colleges in a recent report. The report mentioned that there was a tendency in the early 1970s to reduce institutional requirements for graduation and increasingly to leave such requirements to the discretion of the school or college in which the students were enrolled. One unfortunate result of this trend was a wholesale drop in the requirement of a foreign language for graduation. Only 11 of 148 universities surveyed in 1973 required foreign-language study, and 25 institutions had no university-wide requirements for a baccalaureate degree.

The association predicts that during the 1980s there will be a return to rigorous general educational requirements at the undergraduate level, especially during the first two years. Apparently this movement is already under way on the East and West coasts. It seems that educators throughout the land are returning to a realization that the general education long espoused by Robert Maynard Hutchins, Mortimer J. Adler, and others is necessary for the proper functioning of modern society—especially a democracy. Highly trained but ill-educated specialists cannot get the job done.

All of this raises the question, at least for me, of what an education should do for, or mean to, an individual. Our colleges and universities have been passing through a phase in which technical and professional competence has been stressed almost to the exclusion of other desirable benefits. They now seem to be shifting their emphasis to curricula that will produce more broadly educated graduates with effective citizenship as an objective. But it seems to me that thought needs to be given to a third objective: education that will have meaning to individuals apart from their professional and social responsibilities.

All of this may sound a bit nebulous, but I am sure that all thoughtful individuals struggle with the effort to establish their own identities. Certainly few have ever lived who have not at some time asked, Who and what am I? Why am I? What is my purpose and destiny? The great religions of the world, with their vast literatures, provide evidence that thoughtful people have been concerned with these questions through the ages. The writings of the great philosophers provide similar evidence. The establishment of self-identity and self-esteem may well be the most important goal of successful living.

In my own experience I have frequently been perplexed simply by the existence of matter. Accustomed as I am to thinking in terms of origins, infinite regression ("Who made God?") would appear to make the existence of anything impossible. That elements osmotically extracted from the soil and atmosphere can be constructed into organisms, which for a very brief moment are capable of independent action and even thought, is ultimately incomprehensible.

But if we can trust our senses, matter does indeed exist, with minute portions of it organized into entities that have an awareness of past, present, and future—the power to reflect on what is and what should be. Each entity exists only briefly, in relation to time like the sparks of a welder's torch. However, each rational entity exists long enough to wonder about it all—his or her place and purpose in what many believe must be a universal scheme. Each has a need for self-identity and self-esteem.

During the earlier stages in the development of the human race, perhaps there was less difficulty in achieving these needs. Organized into relatively simple social groups, most individuals could find their places and take pride in their contributions to the whole as leaders, merchants, skilled craftsmen, or what have you. For those who found existence a disappointing experience, some religions provided the concept of a glorious afterlife as solace.

Technological developments have brought about marked changes in our social structure during the twentieth century, many of which I have watched with interest and some dismay. These developments have produced a sort of institutionalization and regimentation that subordinates the individual and tends to destroy or inhibit self-identity and self-esteem. For instance, the faceless workers in a huge automobile assembly plant, each of whom is responsible for only a minute segment of the finished product, are hard put to take pride in their work. They are psychologically smothered by the size of the project in relation to their small input.

The individual is similarly overwhelmed by size in every aspect of his living—labor organizations, educational institutions at all levels, and government agencies. Under these circumstances it is not surprising that the rights of an individual should gradually become subordinate to what is thought to be the welfare of the group as a whole. The concept, basic in Western thought, that individuals have certain natural rights that may not be violated by groups is gradually being dissipated. Individuals are demeaned and demoralized in the process, though they may not understand what is happening. Drifting helplessly like fragments of cork on an ocean wave, they find that their prospects of good lives are limited to finding jobs in which they can earn enough money to purchase a few hours of amusement and a few items of luxury or prestige—meaningless lives that deny them significance. Victimized by the very size of the groups that surround them, they gradually become helpless wards of big government, big labor unions, and big corporations.

With an ever-increasing world population, there seems little likelihood that this trend can be altered or modified to any appreciable extent. Even so, a few individuals have the power to perceive and enjoy through their perceptions. In some, perceptive skills become highly developed and discriminating. Some develop the ability to enjoy intensely the aesthetic experiences made possible by art, music, the theater, and the natural environment.

It seems to me that a major responsibility of our schools at all levels should be to help students develop their potentials for perception to the greatest possible extent. Only then can they fully enjoy the good things about them and develop the capability for rational thought necessary to the solution of problems. This I believe to be the objective of a liberal education—and it is the kind of education from which we began drifting in the 1970s.

From the above you will see why I am much interested

in your comments concerning the recent graduates from our colleges and universities. I surely wish you well in your efforts to revise the curricular offerings and requirements of your institution, especially at the freshman and sophomore levels.

Affectionately,

Serious Problems with Regents

April 24

Dear Bill,

I enjoyed your letter and for the most part agree with your analysis of the relationships that university presidents should have with their governing boards. You are mistaken, however, in thinking that I had no serious problems with the OU board. The following tale should convince you otherwise.

In 1958, J. Howard Edmondson, a young Tulsa attorney, was elected governor of Oklahoma. Despite his youth (he was thirty-three when he took office), Edmondson performed rather well. His most dramatic achievement, as I remember, was the way he ended Prohibition in the state— simply by rigidly enforcing its Prohibition laws.

At first I had no reason to think that the young governor would be troublesome in University affairs. He was a graduate of the OU School of Law, and he had appeared friendly to the University. His first appointee to the Board of Regents was Julian Rothbaum, an attorney of Tulsa, a highly competent individual with an impeccable reputation. Unknown to me, however, trouble was brewing that would come to the surface a few months later.

Early during his second year in office, Edmondson appointed two additional regents—Eph Monroe, a peppery, outgoing attorney from Clinton, to fill the unexpired term of Quintin Little who had resigned, and Dr. Mark R. Johnson, a brilliant physician of Oklahoma City, to succeed Dick Grisso, whose term had expired. I had known Dr. Johnson when he was an undergraduate at OU and was pleased by his appoint-

159

ment. There was still nothing to suggest that I would have any difficulty with the Edmondson administration.

Early in 1961, Edmondson made his fourth appointment to the OU board: James G. Davidson, a Tulsa attorney. Several problems emerged during the following months.

The first had to do with a proposed no-car rule for university freshmen. One of the regents had a daughter who would soon be enrolling in the University, and he didn't want her to have a car. At a regents' meeting early in 1961 a motion was made and seconded that, effective at the beginning of the fall semester, freshmen would not be permitted to have cars at the University. Thinking that such a regulation would be extremely difficult to administer, I protested vigorously and perhaps untactfully. In spite of my objections, the motion passed, though not unanimously. The next day the new regulation was widely publicized by the news media.

Within hours Bud Wilkinson, whose fantastic success as a football coach at OU is well known to you, called me to complain about it. The no-car rule would seriously handicap his recruiting activities, he said. As an example, he mentioned a high-school senior in Wichita Falls—one of the finest quarterback prospects in Texas—who had agreed to come to OU. The boy's parents were giving him an automobile for graduation, and he knew that the boy would not come without his car. Would I see what I could do to get the new rule rescinded?

I told Wilkinson that I had already made myself unpopular with some of the regents by opposing the rule and I was not about to bring up the matter again. I suggested that he talk with Glen Northcutt, of Willis, president of the board, about his problem.

Wilkinson followed my suggestion, and that afternoon I had a phone call from Northcutt asking me to poll the regents by telephone about rescinding their action. In conducting the poll, I found that a majority of the board had changed their minds about the rule, but I did not receive a unanimous vote. Because there was a rule that business could be concluded by telephone only by unanimous vote, it was necessary to take up the matter again at the next meeting of the board. At that time Regent Johnson moved to ignore the result of the telephone poll but to rescind the action establishing the no-car rule. The motion passed. Johnson, Monroe, and Davidson seemed embarrassed and resentful that a regulation of the board should be rescinded so quickly upon the request of the football coach. It was obvious from the conversation that they thought I had used Wilkinson to get the rule changed because I did not like it myself.

Already out of favor with three of Edmondson's appointees, I found myself in further disagreement with them on another matter during the summer of 1961. Early in my administration I had organized an Office of Architectural Planning, headed by Richard Kuhlman. It was Kuhlman's responsibility to work with the departments involved when preliminary plans were prepared for new buildings on the campus. Upon completion of the preliminary plans an architectural firm was employed to prepare the working drawings and supervise the construction of each new building. The architectural fees at that time were 6 percent of the cost of the project. It had been my policy, however, to withhold 1 percent of each fee to pay for the preparation of the preliminary plans under Kuhlman's supervision and pay the remaining 5 percent to the architectural firm that received the contract for the remainder of the project.

Several commercial architectural firms in the state who had supported Edmondson in his race for governor thought that the commercial architects should do all of the work on each new building and receive the entire 6 percent fee. Through the governor, pressure was brought on the regents to discontinue the policy of preparing preliminary plans in Kuhlman's office and assign each project entirely to the commercial architect. I resisted the pressure successfully, but that certainly did not improve my relations with the three most recent appointees to the board. Their hostility toward me was thinly veiled, and they were caustically critical of the university architect and his staff nearly every time reference was made to OU's building program. The other four members of the board remained friendly, but, on occasion I had a feeling that they thought that I could have been more cooperative. I made a mental note to be careful in the future.

In the meantime, there had been interesting political developments that could have caused additional problems for me. During the latter part of 1961 the Edmondson faction began thinking about the next gubernatorial election. Under the Oklahoma Constitution, Edmondson could not succeed himself, and it was necessary to find a candidate who would perpetuate his policies and benefits for his supporters. It was soon decided that Bud Wilkinson, Oklahoma's very successful and esteemed football coach was just the man. Regent Davidson was dispatched to discuss the possibility with him. Unaware, or disdainful, of the regents' policy requiring an employee of the University to resign before running for high public office, Davidson promised Bud that he could have a leave of absence to enter the race and return to his coaching job if he lost. Wilkinson came to me almost immediately and asked if such an arrangement was possible. I told him of the regents' policy, and he expressed agreement with it. The Edmondson supporters, however, continued to regard him as a potential candidate.

A few weeks later Earl Sneed, dean of the College of Law, apparently flirted with the idea of running for governor. At least, the possibility was discussed rather extensively in the newspapers. The thought of Sneed as a possible candidate brought consternation to the Edmondson camp. With both Wilkinson and Sneed in the race, the University-related vote would be split, whereas, solid backing would be needed to nominate Wilkinson. But the Edmondson supporters speedily came up with a solution. Edmondson himself came to see the dean and asked him whether he would like to forget about the governorship and become president of the University of Oklahoma. When Sneed asked what would happen to the incumbent president, the governor replied that something would be found for him—that he would not suffer financially. Sneed reported all of this to me the following day with the assurance that he would not become involved with any move to take over the presidency of the University.

Neither Sneed nor Wilkinson entered the governor's race, but Wilkinson changed his political registration from Democrat to Republican early in 1964 and became a candidate for the United States Senate—only to be defeated by Fred Harris, an OU alumnus.

Early in 1962, a new difficult situation developed. The twenty-eighth session of the Oklahoma legislature had passed a bill creating a Board of Unexplained Deaths but, with characteristic optimism, had failed to appropriate operational funds for it. Shortly thereafter, as a result of political maneuvering, the State Board of Regents for Higher Education was induced to extend the function of the University School of Medicine to permit its cooperation with the Board of Unexplained Deaths—actually, to assume responsibility for its operation. The regents, however, did not allocate funds to cover the cost of the new cooperative arrangement.

The problem was brought to the attention of Regent Johnson, who in turn reported it to the regents of the University at a meeting in early February. Johnson pointed out that there was no money to fund the Board of Unexplained Deaths and that the board pathologist had been serving voluntarily without pay. Johnson thought that the University was morally obligated to find funds to pay for the operations of the board. Regents President Leonard Savage then appointed Regents Johnson and Northcutt to work with me to find the money.

When the three of us met in an effort to solve the problem, Johnson made it clear that he thought there was no money at the School of Medicine available to finance the new program. He asked whether funds could be transferred from the Norman campus to the medical school for the purpose. The amount involved was not large—about $20,000 to $30,000 a year, as I recall—but I thought that the precedent of shifting funds in this fashion, when each campus received a separate allocation from the state regents, was a bad one to set. I explained this to Johnson and Northcutt and suggested that, in any event, the University regents did not have the authority to make the transfer; I thought that only the State Regents for Higher Education had the power to reallocate money.

The matter was held in abeyance until the University board met in May, 1962. At that time Regent Johnson moved that the OU regents send a letter to the state regents requesting authority to transfer funds available on the Norman campus to the medical center. In making the motion, Johnson disregarded the fact that communications between the two boards usually went through the office of the president. This was perhaps fortunate for me, because I was in a rebellious mood at a time that required diplomacy and I probably would have refused to write the letter. A few days later the request was sent over the signature of Dave J. Morgan, who had succeeded Savage as president of the OU regents.

The request came to the attention of the news media from the office of E. T. Dunlap, chancellor of the State System of Higher Education. A reporter friend called me to ask why the transfer was being made, and I explained my position. In the story that appeared, it was pointed out that the proposal was a controversial one—that there was opposition to taking back funds already allocated for campus operations in Norman.

During my years as president I had made it a point to stay on good terms with the news media, especially the news personnel with whom I had regular contacts in Oklahoma City. This effort paid good dividends during the hours following the appearance of the reporter's story. An editorial writer for the *Oklahoma City Times* called me the morning the story appeared and asked for additional information. That afternoon an editorial entitled "OU Regents Wrong" appeared in the *Times.* The opening sentence stated, "The University of Oklahoma board of regents stumbled in recommending an allocation from the university's present budget for the new medical examiner system." The editorial went on to explain that there was no relationship between higher education and the medical-examiner system. The writer added that transferring money for this purpose would take the legislature off the hook so that it would feel no obligation in the future to appropriate funds for the medical-examiner system.

Although I realized that figuratively I was playing a game of Russian roulette, I called the president of our Alumni Association and asked for additional help. The president called a meeting of the association's board, and a few days later a resolution protesting the transfer was sent to Regents President Morgan.

The impact of the news story, the editorial, and the resolution from the alumni caused members of the OU board to withdraw from their support of the transfer of funds. They did not take official action, but the minutes of their regular meeting in June show that the matter was brought up for brief discussion and it was agreed that "no further action was needed." Johnson suspected, with ample justification, that I had tried to sabotage his proposal, and he discussed his suspicions with the other members of the board. As a result, my relations with Johnson, Monroe, and Davidson were strained during the next few months. Hostility varying from covert to overt characterized future meetings. The climax came in December, 1962, when the board held its monthly meeting in Clinton.

Following a dinner and meeting at the Clinton Country Club that evening, members of the board were invited to the home of Regent Monroe for an executive session. I was not present at the meeting, of course, but a friendly member of the board later told me what had happened. During a session that lasted into the small hours of the morning, my inadequacies as president of the University were thoroughly aired by Regents Johnson, Monroe, and Davidson: I had permitted the athletic situation at the University to get out of hand. I had used Wilkinson's influence to bring pressure on the board concerning matters not directly related to athletics—the no-car rule for freshmen, for example. I had been uncooperative with the board in regard to the building program, especially in working with the architects. Members of the board did not receive the courtesies to which they were entitled on the OU campus—three board members had been refused admission to the elevator to the stadium press box because they did not have the required press cards. Three of Edmondson's appointees were convinced that I should be fired, but the fourth, Julian Rothbaum, did not agree. The members did decide, however, that I should be warned to do better in the future. Regents Morgan and Savage were selected to deliver the message to me.

I met with Morgan and Savage the next week in Oklahoma City. They were sympathetic and concerned. They mentioned that Savage's term had expired the preceding spring and that the governor might at any time appoint a successor to him (presumably Joe Cannon, a rising young attorney and supporter of Edmondson), which would make it possible to bring about my dismissal. They assured me that they would try to be helpful in every way possible, but suggested that I stay rather close to my office so that I would be available in case an effort was made to unseat me. Driving home after that session, I reflected that I was in a precarious situation, and I could find only scant comfort in the conviction that I had been right in all the areas of controversy.

With the passage of time my shaken confidence stabilized. The expected announcement that the governor had appointed Joe Cannon to succeed Leonard Savage did not come. Apparently Governor Edmondson, who surely planned to run for the United States Senate sometime, decided that it would be best not to alienate my friends. Henry Bellmon was elected the first Republican governor of the state that fall, and Edmondson passed on to him the responsibility of naming a successor to Savage.

You see from all of this that during one period I did indeed have serious problems with my board. The story may give you comfort as you cope with yours.

Affectionately,

Reconciliation with Regents

Dear Bill,

You're right. I didn't tell the entire story in my last letter. My status *did* remain uncertain until Governor Bellmon actually took office in 1963. There *was* "some problem" about the building of the clubhouse on the golf course. And friendly relations *were* finally established with all of Edmondson's appointees to the OU board.

Perhaps I should explain about cause for concern in the first few days of January, 1963, preceding Bellmon's inauguration.

A few days after Morgan and Savage warned me about my precarious situation, I was told by a lawyer friend that Edmondson had not appointed Cannon to succeed Savage because the governor was prohibited by law from appointing more than four members to the Board of Regents. Much later I learned that there was no such legal prohibition, but for the time being I relaxed.

Then, on January 1, 1963, came the news of the death of Oklahoma's United States Senator Robert S. Kerr from a heart attack. Kerr's death prompted much speculation about what Edmondson would do to fill Oklahoma's vacancy in the Senate. Attention centered on two possibilities: Edmondson could appoint his brother, United States Representative Ed Edmondson, to serve until the next state election. Or the governor could resign, thereby allowing Lieutenant Governor George Nigh to succeed him with the understanding that Nigh would name him to finish out Kerr's term in the Senate. Most Oklahomans thought that Edmondson would maneuver himself into the Senate seat. They were right.

Early in January, 1963, Edmondson resigned as governor, and Nigh took over the post and named Edmondson to succeed Kerr.

At first this interesting political maneuvering seemed relatively unimportant to me. Then my legal-minded friend who thought that a governor was limited to four appointments to the OU board pointed out that Nigh was not under any such restriction. Doubtless, he suggested, Edmondson would arrange with Nigh to replace Savage on the board and finally achieve what he had wanted to do for so long. Some news media speculated that Nigh would make the appointment during his short term as governor. I doubted this, because I thought that Edmondson, facing an election in 1964 to ensure his continuance in the Senate, would not want to be involved, even indirectly, with the firing of the university president. That turned out to be the case.

While, as I have said, I finally established very good relations with the three hostile Edmondson appointees, we were to have one further disagreement—this one over the construction of the clubhouse on the OU golf course.

From time to time during 1962 and 1963, Wilkinson and I discussed the need for a new clubhouse. For several years the University had used a portion of the officer's club on the old South Base, adjacent to the eighteen-hole course. During the years, the building had deteriorated from weathering and termite activity. The locker room, showers, and pro shop were in deplorable condition, and it was obvious that the building should be torn down, if it didn't burn down first.

Because the project was comparatively small, we decided that the University architects would prepare all the plans. As I mentioned in my last letter, the Office of Architectural Planning had survived the pressure to discontinue it, though Kuhlman had resigned because of the caustic criticism he had received. R. C. Dragoo, Jr., his assistant, had succeeded him as head architect.

Plans and working drawings for the facility were completed and presented to the regents at the board's regular meeting on May 14, 1964. The project was approved by a 4 to 3 vote, and the University was authorized to secure bids for construction. Bids were opened on June 25, and it was found that a local construction company had submitted the lowest bid, $239,772.

At the July meeting, from which Regent Houchin was absent, I recommended approval of the low bid. In the vote on a motion to approve my recommendation, Regents Sparks and Johnson abstained; Regents Monroe, Little, and Rothbaum voted aye; and Davidson voted no. Monroe then asked whether, since the proposal had been approved by a vote of only 3 to 1, it was legally possible to proceed with construction; he thought that, because there were seven members of the board, four aye votes were needed. The decision was postponed until the August meeting.

The postponement was interpreted as failure to approve the project by the major state newspapers. One writer suggested that some of the regents had friends who were professional architects and that these friends perhaps resented the fact that university architects had prepared the plans for the building. Another suggested that Wilkinson had initiated the idea of building a golf facility and that the Edmondson appointees on the board were not in a mood to approve anything that Wilkinson favored (I mentioned earlier that Wilkinson was out of favor with the Edmondson faction because he had not only turned down their suggestion that he run for governor as a Democrat, but had changed his registration to Republican early in 1964—he was expected to face Edmondson in the race for the United States Senate that fall). On the campus itself the action was read as a sign that the regents

170

were not ready to approve anything recommended by the president beyond routine matters.

There was perhaps some basis for each of these interpretations, but I think that the regents were honestly concerned about the public-relations consequences of building a clubhouse at the University, even though the project would be supported entirely by athletic revenue—no appropriated funds would be spent on it. Regent Davidson, the most emphatic opponent of the project, took the position that the building was too expensive, implying that the plans provided for a structure that was too luxurious and "plush." He was quoted in the *Tulsa World* as saying that that "La Fortune Park club house, which serves all of the city of Tulsa, was built for far less than that." He was further quoted as saying, "I am willing to use all the persuasion I can to stop this project." Actually, the proposed fieldstone-and-concrete-block building, which totaled 16,855 square feet, was scarcely adequate for the future needs of the university, and in no sense could it be considered luxurious or plush. Under the bid the cost per square foot would have been $14.50, considerably less than the cost per square foot for any building that had recently been constructed or was under construction at the University.

At the August, 1964, meeting, Regent Sparks was absent, but Monroe had his proxy to vote against constructing the building. His proxy, together with the votes of Regents Monroe, Johnson, and Davidson, who had already agreed to vote no, defeated the project. It was agreed that a committee of the board would work with Bob James, manager of the golf course, and Kenneth Farris, athletics business manager, to reduce the size of the building to lower the cost of construction. Noticeably absent from the committee were the athletic director and the University president. During the following months revised plans were prepared eliminating many of the features of the original building and reducing the square footage from 16,855 to 12,716—a 25 percent reduction. Still the regents were reluctant to move on the project, and I, having made two recommendations, decided to let the matter ride. It was not until early spring, 1968, that the board finally decided to advertise for bids. At the April meeting a low bid of $277,950 was accepted. Inflation had taken its predictable toll, and the University received approximately 25 percent less building for a little over $38,000 more money. The moral here is, I suppose, that when the president of the University and the athletic director are not in tune with the governing board it is likely to be costly to the institution—costly in time and money.

In response to your final question, in light of the above it is not even yet clear to me just how or why my relations with the Edmondson appointees to the board improved. Whatever happened, Monroe and Dr. Johnson became my very good friends. During my last three years as president, Cleo and I enjoyed a quail dinner each fall in Monroe's home in Clinton. Dr. Johnson solved a rather complicated health problem for our son Braden and was completely cooperative during my final two years as president. Davidson, while he remained somewhat aloof, permitted his son to enroll in a course that I taught for a few years after I retired from the presidency. Obviously he did not fear any reprisal from me. All's well that ends well.

Affectionately,

On Federal Grants

Dear Bill,

I suspect that many university presidents share your concern about the impact of the federal government on higher education. But with this concern must come the realization that the impact was inevitable—that it came from what were thought to be the nation's needs. Retrospection makes this clear.

Back in the midnineteenth century rapid development in agricultural and industrial activities created a demand for technically competent personnel that could not be met immediately. Congress responded to the need by passing the Morrill Land Grant Act of 1862, and the land-grant-college movement was under way. Impetus was given to the movement by the Hatch Act of 1887, which established agricultural-experiment stations, and by the Second Morrill Act of 1890, which made federal money available for the support of instruction in certain specified industrial and agricultural programs. The success of the movement brought the Smith-Lever Act in 1914, creating the agricultural extension service through the land-grant colleges. Except for the bureaucracy that accompanied it, the impact of the land-grant movement has been favorable.

During the fifth decade of the twentieth century an awareness of a need for additional technically trained personnel developed early in World War II. Impressed by the chilling ingenuity of German scientists and technologists in the production of sophisticated weaponry—especially rocketry—and the possibility of the use of atomic energy in warfare, the federal government realized that the war could be lost through technological inadequacy. This led to government support of several research centers in certain universities—notably the Lincoln Laboratory at MIT, the Lawrence Radiation Laboratory at the University of California, and the Argon at the University of Chicago. Ultimately support was extended to include most major universities through contractual arrangements (grants of money for specified research) with various governmental agencies such as the Department of Health, Education, and Welfare; the Department of Defense; and the National Science Foundation.

The war's end did not bring an end to the perceived need for government-sponsored research. Russia's postwar success with rocketry, spotlighted by the launching of Sputnik in 1957, suggested that the Soviets might gain control of space; the need for increased scientific and technological effort in our own country seemed obvious.

Federal expenditures for research and development increased manyfold—much of the money going to a few leading universities through research grants. Clark Kerr, the president of the University of California, in *The Uses of the University,* states that by 1960 higher education was receiving approximately $1.5 billion from the federal government—"a hundredfold increase in twenty years."

All of this had an enormous impact, certainly not always for the good, on the nation's universities. The huge sums of money available for research caused intense competition for faculty immediately after the war, at a time when academic researchers were in short supply and enrollments were growing dramatically.

It was only natural, I suppose, that a relatively few of the prestigious institutions, both public and private, received most of the research grants. To quote Kerr once again, "Washington did not waste its money on the second rate." It was perhaps natural also that the favored institutions freely raided the scientific talent of less fortunate institutions. I know that the University of Oklahoma suffered from this competition because of its inadequate salary budget. During the postwar years we were able to recruit many very promising young scientists, only to lose them to federally financed projects after they had demonstrated their competence. In my speeches about the state I occasionally referred to the University of Oklahoma as an "academic boot camp."

While there is little doubt that federal money greatly strengthened the research programs of the country's leading institutions, there were several less desirable effects. Probably the most widespread ill effect was that, with the best scientific talent in the country heavily engaged in research and administering research grants, undergraduate instruction in practically all institutions suffered neglect.

Another item in the debit column of the balance sheet is that any institution that receives federal grants must lose a measure of control over its activities. Grants are made through individuals and are not subject to budgeting by the institution. In addition, the possessor of a grant may be in a position to exert undue pressure on his institution with respect to several matters, including the assignment of space. If he doesn't get what he thinks he needs, he can move to another institution and take his grant with him. This, I think, has led to some undesirable consequences, including the waste of grant money—the purchase of unneeded equipment, collusion among grant holders in spending grant money for "consultative services," and the occasional diversion of grant money to purposes not related to the approved project, to mention a few.

Another adverse effect is that the federal agencies making the grants decide what research will be supported. From personal experience at the University of Oklahoma I know that the real research interests of some young researchers have been cast aside for projects for which there is assurance of federal funding. They have "decided" to become interested in related projects for which federal money is available. It seems apparent to me that researchers do their best work when they are involved in projects of primary interest. Research projects that are undertaken because financing is available are often of doubtful worth.

I have been disturbed also about the impact of grants on faculty loyalties. When I was a member of the OU faculty, and even during most of my tenure as president, departmental faculties were close-knit groups. With only occasional exceptions, each individual felt loyalty to his or her discipline, department, college, and the university as a whole. With the advent of grants and grantsmanship, the situation has changed greatly. Many grant recipients have no such loyalties. Their loyalties are primarily to the sources of their grants—the agencies in Washington that distribute the money. They often feel closer to federal personnel than to their colleagues on campus. You are, of course, aware of this, and you are rightly disturbed by what is going on in your own institution.

Several presidents with whom I have talked in recent years ruefully admit that they wish federal grants had never been made available to their faculty members, or at least that they had not been awarded for specific projects. I think probably all would agree that it would have been better if the grants had been made to the institutions, without restrictions, for use in developing research potential on their campuses. But probably no president has been naïve enough to believe that when something is given nothing will be expected in return.

Reading Kerr's book, I was amused by a limerick that he quoted, credited to a Professor Don Price:

On Federal Grants

There was a young lady from Kent
Who said that she knew what it meant
When men took her to dine, gave her cocktails and wine;
She knew what it meant—but she went.

Kerr commented that he wasn't sure that the universities and their presidents always knew what it meant when their faculty members received grants, "But one thing is certain—they went."

You can see that I share your concern about the impact of the federal government on our nation's colleges and universities. But I see no lessening of that impact until federal funds are made available without strings—an unlikely prospect.

Affectionately,

Student Attitudes

May 25

Dear Bill,

Fifteen years ago I would have thought that I had an answer to your question, "Why do student attitudes vary so much from time to time—almost in relation to decades?" I am no longer sure; I can only speculate. I readily concede that student attitudes during the 1970s were vastly different from those of the 1960s. It is interesting to look back through the decades.

Until the twentieth century American university students were not frequently inclined to be critical of what is now known as "the establishment," though they were sometimes at odds with faculties or administrations. Possibly their acquiescence was related to the elitism of the academic communities during the early years of American higher education. Students came to universities from privileged backgrounds—largely from families of means—to prepare for the professions—law or medicine—or for theology. Perhaps they saw little need to think of education in terms of social problems. Only those directly involved in a problem are likely to see need for reform.

Soon after the turn of the century, with growing college-student populations, the elitism of higher education began to disappear. Students from less-privileged backgrounds gradually increased, narrowing the gap between college students and the youth of the country as a whole. This seems to have changed the thinking on many campuses. For example, during the first decade of the new century students showed a new interest in social problems, especially labor problems, an interest expressed in the organization of chapters of the

Intercollegiate Socialist Society on a great many campuses throughout the country. The members believed that socialism was the answer to several problems, including the sweatshops of the East and the insatiable greed of the robber barons.

The plight of working men and women certainly needed attention during that period. Despite the best efforts of Samuel Gompers and his American Federation of Labor, organized back in the 1880s, little progress had been made to improve the welfare of the working class. My good friend Dave McKown, a prominent Oklahoma City insurance executive, once told about a depressing experience his father had had back in 1907. The senior McKown was part of a carpentry crew constructing a superstructure for a mining company in Illinois. A steel beam slipped and crushed one of his legs below the knee. Although fellow workers helped him to his horse and buggy, company officials made no effort to provide assistance—made no arrangements to see that he got home safely. He had to crawl from the buggy to his house, where he was incapacitated for weeks without income and with a wife and three children to support. There was no workmen's compensation in those days—no unemployment benefits, no Social Security. It is difficult to see how a family could survive under such circumstances, even with relatives and friends coming to the rescue.

During and after World War I organized student groups voiced vigorous antiwar sentiments—they were especially opposed to postwar military training at colleges and universities. This attitude persisted into the second and third decades.

I can cite an interesting example from the second decade. OU's distinguished ornithologist, the late George Miksch Sutton, who ranked among the best in his field and certainly was the country's premier bird artist, was attending Bethany College, in West Virginia, and was to graduate in 1919. World

War I ended during the fall of his senior year, but Bethany decided to establish a student Army training corps that year.

Sutton, who was president of the student body, and twelve others objected unsuccessfully to the "militarization" of their institution—seeing no need for such activity with the ending of the war. Although Sutton participated in the required program and even advanced to the rank of corporal, he and his fellow students continued to be vocal in their objections. Finally all thirteen were dismissed from school.

For a time after his dismissal the young rebel was philosophical about missing out on a bachelor's degree; he could still live his life as he wished—studying and painting birds. Only the possibility of employment as an ornithologist, at the Carnegie Museum in Pittsburgh revived his interest in academics. He applied for and was granted readmission to Bethany and, working part time finally completed the requirements for a degree in 1923.

A doctor of science degree from Cornell University in 1932, followed by twenty years of distinguished ornithological research, again brought him to the attention of his alma mater. In 1952 Bethany awarded him an honorary doctorate of science. While it might be considered a gracious gesture, it did not make up for the years of productive life lost through his dismissal in 1919. To top it off, the president of Bethany, in conferring the doctorate, mispronounced Sutton's admittedly difficult middle name, referring to him as George "Mikiskey" Sutton. But Sutton was philosophical about it all—and pleased that his name was correctly spelled on the diploma.

Sutton and the others at Bethany, of course, objected to the inclusion of military training in the curriculum on idealistic grounds. My objection to similar training when I entered South Dakota State College in the fall of 1923 was based on the fact that two mornings each week I had to wrap several feet of wrappings around each leg so that I would be properly uniformed for those days. I was not clever at this, and my leggings frequently came loose during the day. But unlike Sutton, I voiced no protest. I felt fortunate to be in college, and it would never have occurred to me to criticize institutional requirements.

During the fourth decade the Great Depression that followed the economic crash of 1929, with resulting record-breaking unemployment, made even more acute in our part of the country by several years of drought, had a devastating impact not only on the country's student population but on all the youth. How well I remember those days! My salary at the University of South Dakota was reduced by one third between 1930 and 1933, and I was making less than $2,000 a year when the opportunity I had to move to the University of Oklahoma came in 1934. It was a most difficult period, and on college campuses former causes, such as labor abuses and militarism, were overshadowed by a widespread belief that something was basically wrong with the structure and fabric of our government. This, of course, led to the political rebellion that unseated the Republican party and brought Franklin D. Roosevelt to the presidency of the United States.

The generation that grew to maturity during the Depression could be characterized more by realism than idealism. Justifiable feelings of insecurity narrowed their objectives to the learning of skills that would enable them to make a living, to accumulate resources that would provide security for their families, and to achieve whatever socioeconomic status possible under the circumstances. Life for all but a favored few was pretty much a grind, with scant leisure to ponder ways and means of bettering relationships among the segments of our complicated social structure. Lack of time to consider such matters left the generation poorly equipped to understand the thinking and behavior of their sons and daughters who would be teenagers during the 1960s.

During the fifth decade World War II brought a dramatic end to the Great Depression and ushered in a period of unparalleled prosperity—an affluence never before or since experienced by any nation. Unemployment virtually disappeared during the war; the only unemployed were the unemployable. As you doubtless remember, even after the war unemployment was not a serious matter. The GI Bill largely took up the slack by making it possible for thousands of returning servicemen and women to attend colleges, universities, and other institutions of learning or training. Amazing technological advances, plus what seemed to be an inexhaustible supply of cheap energy, stimulated industrial development and ensured employment for practically everyone who wanted to work. The objectives for which the Depression generation had striven under most discouraging circumstances became easily available.

Thus children born to families during the late fifth and early sixth decades knew little of want or privation. They already had what their parents had worked so hard to gain. With a superabundance of good things—even a surfeit—the emerging generation became bored and dissatisfied. This, plus the Vietnam War, according to many sociologists, led to the hippie age and the confrontations in academe of the seventh decade.

The youth of that decade, as you will recall, were most adept at discovering wrongs that needed to be righted. Suspecting an unholy coalition of the military, industry, and government that they called "the establishment" many of them became antagonistic toward practically everything that went on in society. On the campuses resentment toward military training was extended to include other institutional requirements, with charges of repression, regimentation, and hypocrisy. The evils of racism became a featured issue. They found ample reason for rebellion at a great many universities, which, they charged, were geared to prepare them for a way of life that had proved a failure.

The events that led to the violence of the 1960s began toward the end of the preceding decade, and they involved the off-campus activities of students, especially those at the University of California—to influence legislation and legislative committee deliberations. In an effort to keep the students on campus, as you may recall, President Kerr issued a series of directives designed to reduce or control off-campus activity in late 1959. The directives were unsuccessful. In 1960 hundreds of students were fire-hosed when they demonstrated against the House Committee on Un-American Activities on the steps of the City Hall in San Francisco. This incident and others did little to put the students in a frame of mind to accept an administrative decision in 1964 to ban campus meetings related to certain off-campus causes. The demonstrations that followed, including the occupation of Sproul Hall, grew in violence and spread to other institutions. Kerr, as we all recall with regret, lost his job.

Why there should have been a reversal of student attitudes during the early 1970s is anyone's guess. With the exception of a minor recession or two there was no significant change in the country's economy. Good things were available in abundance without anything approaching the effort needed during the Depression years. Many have regarded the Vietnam War as a major contributing factor to the unrest of the sixties. But the change in attitude was apparent before the war ended. Perhaps the new crop of teenagers regarded the hippie era as an experiment that failed. Or there may be a sort of periodicity in the thinking of teenagers, with waves and troughs, so to speak. In any event, as you say, there is an entirely different attitude on university campuses today, expressed by an obvious effort to prepare for the professions—especially business. The increasing number of candidates for the degree of master of business administration at OU has been interesting. I understand that this is happening throughout the country.

If you are interested in a thorough analysis of student attitudes in the country through the first seven decades of the century, I suggest you obtain a copy of *The Student and the University,* by Elvin Abeles (published in 1969 by the Parents Magazine Press of New York). Although it is very well written, the book did not sell as well as it should have, handicapped by an unimaginative title and a drawing of a clenched fist above marching students on the jacket. Besides analyzing student attitudes, the author presents a very readable account of the history of universities from ancient times to the present. It is well worth your reading.

Affectionately,

P.S. One more thought about the changes that have taken place in employer-employee relations since the time of McKown's accident so long ago: During the century the success of labor unions in improving the lot of the laboring class certainly has been dramatic. Some think that the pendulum may have swung too far—that the unions have become too powerful. Some credence was given this thought recently when the Professional Air Traffic Controllers organization saw fit to challenge the laws of the United States and go out on strike.

I do not consider such ill-advised action an indictment of the much-needed union movement. It is, rather, an indictment of union leadership.

In historical retrospect, it would appear that the human race is inherently incapable of maintaining a balanced, stable situation because of the greed of the leaders who have emerged.

The unfit working conditions provided by the equally power-ful industrialists before the unions were organized were in-tolerable for those who were forced to work there. With the advent of unions the selfish goals of those in power have prevented the development of an equitable accommodation. Power, almost inevitably accompanied by greed, may be the Achilles' heel of human relationships. It may be no wonder that thoughtful youth periodically become impatient with us.

Special Programs

Dear Bill,

You are right that I take great pride in two special programs developed at the University of Oklahoma—the Center for Continuing Education and the University of Oklahoma Press. I regard the Center for Continuing Education as among the very best of its kind in the country, and during the later years of my administration *Time* magazine called the Press one of the three best university presses in the nation. The answer to your question, "How were you able to develop such excellence in these two programs with such limited financial resources?" is easy to answer. It was a matter of finding the right people to provide leadership in developing them. Money, though necessary in at least minimal amounts for the success of any enterprise, is never the main ingredient. Imagination, innovation, and drive are the determining factors. In my opinion, too much money often can provide a handicap.

You will surely want to do everything possible to continue the development of your own extension division, but I am not sure that you should attempt to expand your publishing activities to the status of a press in the sense that the term is used in the major universities. Another university in your state has an established press. Your institution, a four-year college advanced to university status only a few years ago, would be ill-advised to launch an expensive publishing program. Throughout the country universities appear to be having difficulty financing their presses. In view of the fact that a university press exists to provide an avenue for the publication of scholarly books and journals that deserve publication but would not be regarded as profitable ventures by a commercial press, it is not realistic to assume that it can be self-sustaining. A university press must have financial support from sources other than its earnings—in a state-supported university, from appropriated funds.

An extension division is quite a different matter. Properly managed, it can be self-supporting. After receiving your letter, I checked briefly into the history of our center at OU. It had its beginnings in 1911 or 1912 in a committee of the faculty organized to furnish speakers for various events—high-school commencements and other community programs—throughout the state. In 1913 the scope of the program was expanded after the state legislature established two extension departments in the University—the Department of Extension Lectures and the Department of Public Information and Welfare. Through the latter department various activities were added to the program—public discussion, debate, and correspondence study.

The two departments operated as separate entities until 1923, when all extension activities were consolidated under the director of University Extension.

In 1933, in the midst of the Depression, it was necessary to reduce the extension activities drastically. Several were discontinued, and only a skeleton staff was retained. The name Division of University Extension was changed to Division of Public Relations. The new name was used for only three years, however; in 1936, the earlier name, slightly revised, University Extension Division, was reinstated without any change in services.

With the lessening of the Depression in the late 1930s several new programs were added, including extension courses broadcast over WNAD, the University's radio station, which had been established back in 1923; a visual-education service; and the Oklahoma Family-Life Institute (it is perhaps worth mentioning that WNAD is believed to have been the first university broadcasting station in the country).

The real flowering of the extension program came, however, during the years following World War II. With the war's closing, the University acquired the naval air station north of Norman. The extension division was moved from its cramped quarters in Old Science Hall to the very spacious enlisted men's recreation hall and the officers' clubhouse on the station. Thurman White, who had been added to the extension staff in 1941, returned after a tour of duty with the Marines to succeed Boyd Gunning as director of extension activities. The very capable and versatile Gunning became director of the University of Oklahoma Foundation and secretary of the Alumni Association. The new quarters, presided over by a very innovative, energetic new director, made possible rapid developments—I remember with some amusement the remodeling of the officers' bar into a conference room and the rapidly increasing number of sessions that were held there.

These facilities for extension could only be regarded as temporary, however, and it was necessary to look to the future for permanent housing. During the late 1950s, White came up with the idea that a grant might be obtained from the W. K. Kellogg Foundation, to help build a new center on the south side of the main campus. He had visited the outstanding extension facility constructed with Kellogg aid at Michigan State College, and he had heard that the foundation was in the mood to make an additional grant to some institution for such a purpose.

We knew, of course, that there would be intense competition for money of this kind. White, working with the University architect, drew up a set of plans and constructed a model that might interest the president of the foundation and his associates. The plans called for a decentralized design—a Forum Building, a Hall for Advanced Studies, a hotel, an administration building, and ten duplex cottages for the use of participants in extended conferences.

When everything was in readiness, we made an appointment to see the president of the foundation. The visitation party consisted of a member of the board of regents, White, the university architect, and me, as well as the plans and the model for the proposed new center. We decided to fly to Battle Creek, Michigan, in two four-passenger planes. We took off hopeful but prepared to face disappointment, because Kellogg had announced that only one grant would be made and we had heard that several prestigious institutions were also applying for it.

When we arrived at the foundation office, our initial impression was that the president was at best only mildly interested in our proposal—willing to talk with us mostly out of courtesy. When we showed him the model, however, with its decentralized features, his interest grew perceptibly. When we stressed that we did not want to build a hotellike facility but envisioned a community of buildings, he gave most careful attention to our plans, and we left Battle Creek with the feeling that we might indeed receive the hoped-for grant. On the flight home our spirits were not dampened by a severe thunderstorm that forced our two little planes to make unscheduled landings at an isolated airport with grass runways.

Not long afterward came a welcome communication from the Kellogg Foundation that OU would receive a grant of $1.845 million for the center, contingent upon the University's providing a like amount. The matching requirement could be met in part by the contribution of the land to be used, and only $1.3 million in cash would be required. Governor J. Howard Edmondson agreed to help persuade the legislature to supply the matching funds.

The 1959 legislature proved to be a bit difficult to persuade, no doubt partly because a member of the OU faculty had recently referred to the legislators as a group of professional idiots. Finally $650,000 was appropriated—half the needed amount. It appeared that we might have to wait until the next session of the legislature to obtain the rest of the appropriation and claim the Kellogg money. The Kellogg people were understanding, however; they agreed to permit construction with the University's assurance that, should the remainder of the matching money not be made available through legislative channels, the University would issue bonds for it. We broke ground in September, 1959.

At the next session of the legislature the governor submitted a request for the rest of the matching money. After several days of persuasion and debate, the legislators reluctantly passed a bill providing that $325,000 of the remaining matching money should be made available from an "anticipated surplus" in the state's revenues and that the final $325,000 should come from an "unanticipated surplus"—a very bleak prospect. Everyone was greatly surprised when both the anticipated surplus and the unanticipated surplus indeed accrued. The center was finally completed, though at a cost higher than we had anticipated. As I recall, the total ran well over $4 million; we obtained the extra money from the issuance of self-liquidating bonds.

With the magnificent new center as a base for his operations Thurman White was able to develop one of the best programs of its kind in the country, eventually becoming international in scope. The name Extension Division was changed to the Oklahoma Center for Continuing Education. Especially noteworthy was a new program called Liberal Studies, which led to a University degree. This program became a model for other institutions; it attracted many visitors to the campus who wanted to see how it operated.

From the above, you can see that the University of Oklahoma's success in continuing education has been due largely to the genius of Thurman White—his innovativeness in conceiving new programs and his ability to select people qualified to implement them.

With respect to the University of Oklahoma Press, two great directors brought it to international prominence. Joseph A. Brandt, who launched the program in 1929, was uniquely successful in attracting high-quality manuscripts from gifted writers and in providing the editorial services necessary to prepare the manuscripts for publication. By the time he resigned in 1938 to accept the directorship of the University of Princeton Press, the OU Press had achieved respect throughout the country and abroad.

Savoie Lottinville, who had joined the Press staff in 1932, succeeded Brandt as director. Building on Brandt's foundation, with equal vision and innovative effort he brought the Press to a zenith of excellence during the mid-1960s, shortly before his retirement. Brandt and Lottinville well illustrate the principle that the quality of any program is determined by the competence of the one who directs it.

It is the responsibility of the director of a university press to see that manuscripts for publications are selected with discrimination and that the manuscripts are edited by skillful editorial staff to prepare them for publication. Few if any manuscripts are ready for publication as submitted. The director is responsible also for the organization and supervision of an efficient production department, with marketing and sales departments to distribute the product. These diverse responsibilities call for an individual with extraordinarily versatile mental ability—a quality not in plentiful supply. An outstanding university press adds luster to its institution and its authors. Perhaps someday, when the time is right, a press may grace your institution. May you have the good fortune to find a Brandt or a Lottinville to launch it.

Affectionately,

Private Gifts—A Word of Caution

June 20

Dear Bill,

Your letter, written after the completion of your first year as a university president, took me back through time to my own first year as president of the University of Oklahoma. I was reminded of parallel problems and events, though my first year was spent in a quite different setting—World War II. One of my first reactions to your letter was that you have been giving too much attention to what you failed to accomplish during your first year. You have every reason to be proud of what you accomplished.

The failure to develop a foundation, or other independent agency, to receive and manage gifts of money and property to your institution should not cause you great concern. From what you say, you are well along with plans that can be implemented early in your second year. It took six years to develop a plan at the University of Oklahoma.

Back in the 1930s, President William Bennett Bizzell became aware of the potential for private giving to OU. The university had received a substantial gift from the Phillips Petroleum Company to establish the Phillips Collection in Western History. Lew Wentz, an independent oilman, had given the University a generous amount to establish a loan fund for students. Bizzell reasoned that such gifts might be forthcoming more readily if potential donors could be assured that their contributions would not be subject to the political controls thought to be inherent in state universities. His governing board apparently agreed, for in the spring of 1938 it was announced that the University of Oklahoma Foundation would be created to receive and manage private offerings.

193

The foundation was not activated, however; there were no declaration of trust, articles of incorporation, bylaws, or personnel. There is no mention of the foundation in the regents' minutes.

When Brandt succeeded Bizzell in 1941, he took steps to activate the foundation. He recommended inviting an outstanding business leader, Shelley Tracy, of the class of 1911, to get foundation activities under way. After approving his suggestion, the regents named a four-man committee of the board to develop a procedure for activating the foundation. The committee, working with characteristic lack of dispatch, did not get around to reporting until January, 1944, just after I took over as acting president. At that time the committee chairman recommended a "declaration of trust" for the establishment of the University of Oklahoma Foundation, which, after extensive discussion, was approved. It was still many months before the final details of the new agency's operations were worked out. So you need not be discouraged with your failure to get a full-fledged operation under way in one year. In future years you may be very pleased with your initial efforts.

A few weeks ago I noticed articles in local papers reporting that the University of Oklahoma Foundation now has assets totaling more than $40 million. This represents an average growth of $1 million a year since the board approved the trust agreement back in 1941. I was pleased to note also that the endowment portion of the foundation's assets were in excess of $22 million and that during the past five years approximately $30 million had been spent in support of University projects and programs.

Reading the articles carefully, I realized that, while I had been involved with the foundation during its earlier years, its great growth had occurred since I retired—an increase of 303 percent during the past five years. The future looks very promising for the foundation and, therefore, for the University. This is due to the fortunate circumstance of a fossil-fuel boom in Oklahoma combined with a fund-raising genius as president of the University.

The substantial gifts that your institution has already received for various purposes augur well for the ultimate success of your effort. The gift of $1 million from a family to help build an addition to your school of music should be especially reassuring; in most institutions it would be possible to obtain that amount only for a program such as engineering or business administration. The donors' desire to have a part in planning some of the details of the addition should not cause you too much concern as long as they do not try to influence the selection or retention of faculty.

However, I must admit the validity of your concern that large gifts by single donors may occasionally cause a problem if the donor tries to influence the university in some way that is not compatible with the institution's purposes and responsibilities. An extreme example of this, which had far-reaching consequences, occurred at Stanford University near the turn of the century.

As you know, Stanford was founded and during its earlier years supported largely through the munificence of Leland Stanford, who had amassed a fortune in various activities, principally railroads. After his death continued support of the new university was assured through the creation of the Stanford Trust, with his widow, Jane Lathrop Stanford, as sole trustee.

In 1900, a member of the Stanford faculty, Edward A. Ross, spoke publicly on several occasions in support of free silver, a ban on Oriental immigration, municipal ownership of utilities, and an investigation of the Southern Pacific Railroad. Word of Ross's views reached Mrs. Stanford, who, because of her husband's relations with railroads, was understandably displeased. She asked President David Starr Jordan to dismiss Ross from the faculty on the grounds that it would be in the best interests of "her university." Because she controlled the purse-strings of the Stanford Trust, Jordan found it expedient to do what she asked, and Ross lost his job.

The incident was costly to Stanford University, but it did have one good effect: many believe that it was a major factor in the formation of the American Association of University Professors. Several prominent members of the Stanford faculty resigned in protest over Ross's firing and found positions elsewhere. In 1910 one of them, Arthur Oncken Lovejoy joined the Department of Philosophy in Johns Hopkins University. Apparently Lovejoy never forgot the injustice done to Ross. During his tenure at Johns Hopkins he frequently discussed with his colleagues the lack of professionalism throughout the country in the handling of faculty appointments—especially in the dismissal of faculty members. In the spring of 1913 he composed a letter that he and eighteen other full professors in Johns Hopkins sent to colleagues of equal rank in nine other leading universities. The letter suggested the formation of a national organization of professors and invited cooperation in the effort. The appeal was successful: it led to the organization of the American Association of University Professors in January, 1915, with six hundred professors from various institutions as charter members.

The Stanford incident and its aftermath, as well as several lesser instances of donor meddling that could be mentioned, give rise to questions that deserve careful thought. If I were again president of a public university, I think that I would prefer receiving relatively modest contributions from a large number of givers rather than large amounts from a relative few. It would be difficult, of course, to refuse large gifts, unless they were accompanied by compromising conditions.

In your own case, to retain as much independence of action as possible, I suggest that you never accept large personal favors from any of your major donors. Wealthy individuals are inclined to be very generous to those they like. Acts of generosity give them a feeling of importance that they cannot experience any other way. But accepting such largesse imposes an obligation on the receiver that may prove embarrassing later. The timeworn statement "There is no such thing as a free lunch" certainly applies to college presidents. To accept expensive personal favors of any kind could make it embarrassing for a president to say no to some future proposal that is not compatible with his university's mission. Every president should realize that his institution, public or private, exists for the welfare of all of the people, not only for the fortunate few who acquire great wealth. But I am sure that you have thought of these things and that your best judgment will prevail in any situation.

On rereading the above, I have the impression that I may have done an injustice to past large donors to educational institutions by making a bad example (Stanford) seem to be the norm rather than one difficult case. There are, as you doubtless know, many other examples in which major contributors changed the destiny of single institutions—Duke, Rice, Vanderbilt, Chicago, Colorado College, Emory—and I hope that you will not derive from my letter a negative reaction that will make you uneasy in accepting large gifts to your institution made under proper circumstances. Large gifts may be accepted with qualifying conditions, but it should always be clear that the utilization of the gifts will be left to the administration and governing board of the institution. Personal gifts of any substantial value should never be accepted.

Finally, I congratulate you on a most successful first year. Reading between the lines of your last letter, however, I got the impression that you are experiencing feelings of frustration—a hint of doubt that additional years will be rewarding and bring fulfillment. In my own case, after careful retrospection, I am able to assure you that being president of a university, even for a prolonged period, can indeed be a rewarding experience. What could be more satisfying than to have a part in developing the greatest natural resource of our state and country—providing educational opportunities for the nation's youth? Of course, agonies and disappointments have been experienced through the years, but they have been more than matched by the triumphs and satisfactions of seeing the "products" of the institution become effective participants of our social framework—many to achieve distinction in business, industry, and social service.

Perhaps the secret of gaining composure in a job of this kind is to cultivate the ability to attain perspective in every situation.

When I was invited to make a few comments at William S. Banowsky's inauguration as the eighth president of the University in 1978, I suggested the following:

> The various groups represented here today, from within the state and without, have been unanimous in wishing you well. That is good. But I should warn you that this is probably the only time they will agree on any matter during your administration. There will be difficulties—when the honeymoon ends, as it will; when besetting problems seem insurmountable, as they frequently will, and from time to time you wonder why you ever got involved with the situation; and to cap it off, when the football team loses two games in a single season, heaven forbid; when these things happen, in the parlance of the sixties—don't lose your cool, ignore expediency, do your job as you see it, and let the critics howl! And when I can help, let me know.

If one can retain perspective in all situations and avoid over-reacting, the routine of administration will be simplified, and problems will be solved with less stress on the administrator and the staff.

I hope that we can be in touch again this fall when you return from your trip to Africa and the Greek Islands. Have fun during the summer. My love to Diane and the children.

Affectionately,

Appendices

Postwar Educational Problems

(SPEECH DELIVERED AT FACULTY CLUB DINNER, FEBRUARY 23, 1944)

When I was asked to make a few comments this evening, I accepted with considerable reluctance. I have been acting president of the University of Oklahoma for only a month and a half, and it will be obvious to most of you that I am not in a position to present much of value concerning current educational problems. Nevertheless, despite my lack of experience and familiarity with administrative responsibility at the higher levels, I find that I am expected to speak with assurance, if not authority, about practically any phase of the University's operations.

Much is being said and written about educational problems—especially about plans for postwar education. Unfortunately, we are unable to see over the hill, and in these unpredictable days when it is difficult to plan even from week to week, it is obviously much more difficult to plan intelligently for the postwar days. However, we can be certain of one thing: there will be a number of problems concerning education that will need to be solved. It occurred to me that I might bring up a few this evening and discuss them briefly without attempting to provide answers.

One question very much in evidence at the University of Oklahoma—and I presume elsewhere—involves prerequisites for admission to the institution and its diverse curricula of instruction. At the moment, an entering freshman must have completed certain prescribed units of instruction in high school to be admitted to the freshman class. Additional requirements, in many instances, are imposed by the various professional schools and colleges. To be admitted to the Graduate College, a student must have received a bachelor's degree from an accredited college or university and must have included in his undergraduate program a number of prescribed courses, including work in English, mathematics, science, and the social sciences. When the student is admitted, he finds that many courses must be taken in sequence—that certain courses are prerequisites for others.

This bookkeeping method of determining fitness for admission to courses and educational programs has been criticized seriously by many prominent educators, and perhaps the question is really deserving of serious study. Unfortunately, the courses previously taken by a student have not proved to be a reliable indication of his ability to proceed with advanced work. Many feel that we should disregard the student's record of course work almost entirely and determine, through the use of achievement tests, his ability to do the work necessary in a program of study.

Dean Howard M. Jones, of the Harvard Graduate School, would extend this idea even to the graduate level and admit to the graduate college all students who can be found by appropriate tests to be proper candidates for graduate work, regardless of whether or not they have completed programs leading to the bachelor's degree. The trend toward this approach to prerequisites and admission requirements is too powerful to be ignored. I do not pretend to know what should be done. I merely raise the question, which I hope to pass on to the Faculty Senate for consideration. If changes in our present plan prove to be desirable, we should make them. We should not find ourselves guilty of the accusation made recently by the president of a great midwestern university, namely, that "a university faculty is a gigantic conspiracy to maintain the status quo."

Another problem, closely related to the one that I have just mentioned, involves aptitude testing and career counseling. By way of background, we might examine the procedures that have been used here in the past. The high-school graduate begins his university career with what is known as "Freshman Week." After two or three crowded days of meetings, speeches, and other debilitating experiences, he is finally given "placement tests" in certain subjects that are considered basic in the educational process. The tests are given at a time when he is exhausted both physically and mentally, but the results are used, nevertheless, in planning his first enrollment in the University. Many students and their parents think the tests are unfair and discriminatory. The problem needs attention.

I will admit that tests of various kinds are necessary to determine the level at which a student shall begin his university experiences, but I think that they should be given before the student comes to the University—perhaps in the spring of his senior year in high school. Moreover, they should be given, I think, by some agency other than the University—perhaps by the State Board of Regents for Higher Education. The results could then be made available to any of the higher institutions, though they would be identified with none. Under this plan the beginning student could enter the University under pleasant circumstances, without the mental stress that we impose at present, and get off to a much better start. Or, after receiving the results of his tests, he might decide not to enter the University at all.

I would like to see developed at the University an elaborate system of aptitude tests, to be given leisurely during the first semester of a student's enrollment—an enrollment which I think, incidentally, should consist largely of basic courses from the College of Arts and Sciences. The results of the aptitude tests should be made available immediately to a well-trained, interested, and sympathetic adviser who would study them carefully. During this first semester the adviser should become well acquainted with the student and, if possible, with the student's parents and attempt to gain their confidence and friendship. Tests have been developed that measure with considerable validity a dozen or so of the basic aptitudes, and it is possible to determine with reasonable certainty what a student can or cannot be expected to do successfully.

With the information concerning the student's aptitudes, the adviser could, if he had gained the confidence of the student, do much during the second semester of the freshman year to steer the student toward the profession or other activity in which he would be most likely to succeed. One way to do it would be to encourage the student to engage in activities or take elective courses designed to utilize his aptitudes and arouse an interest in the profession for which his aptitudes best seem to fit him. In most instances I believe that it should be possible for the student to choose and enter a professional school at the beginning of the sophomore year.

There are many difficulties involved in putting this plan into effect. A group of absolutely impartial advisers, who would reject any idea of professional proselyting, would have to be selected—not easy to do. Then there would be budgetary difficulties. Nevertheless, I believe that the development of an advisory system of this type should be the primary objective of the University College in the future.

Another matter of considerable importance is that of providing training for our returning ex-servicemen. I think that two problems will emerge in this connection.

The first of these stems from the fact that those returning from the war probably will feel that they should receive college or university credit for the in-service educational training that they received with the armed forces. They will feel that their experiences have been worth something in terms of high-school or college credits.

206

The American Council on Education has anticipated this attitude, and the U.S. Armed Forces Institute, with headquarters in Madison, Wisconsin, has been set up to help educational institutions cope with it in the postwar period. However, a false impression of the functions of the U.S. Armed Forces Institute apparently has developed, namely that the institute will evaluate, in terms of high-school and college credits, the in-service educational training of each individual released from the armed forces. This is not the case. The institute will, upon application, furnish to each educational institution an accurate record of the in-service training and mental development of each ex-service individual who may apply for admission to a particular school or college after he is released from the service. This information will consist of valid records and measures of educational attainments and competency but will not be in the form of units or semester hours of credit to which the individual is entitled as a result of his experiences. The information is intended to be of practical aid to the institution in evaluating the educational experiences of the ex-servicemen, but it will be up to each institution to determine just how much credit may be allowed for these experiences.

Unfortunately, there are now signs of a wide divergence of opinion and practice concerning the granting of credit for training received while in the military service. If this continues, it is probable that ex-servicemen may want to shop around a bit and find a school or college that will award them the largest amount of credit for their military experiences. This, of course, would be unfortunate, and I hope that the higher institutions will develop fairly uniform practices with respect to the granting of such credits. Perhaps at least in Oklahoma the schools will work together in a cooperative effort to solve the problem for this area.

The returning ex-servicemen will probably ask credit

for diverse types of training too numerous to be enumerated here. Certainly the question of credit for basic military training, officer-candidate training, training in technician schools, correspondence courses taken through the U.S. Armed Forces Institute, and various types of vocational work will be submitted. To aid in this confusing situation, the American Council on Education proposes to set up a special committee to prepare a manual describing the programs in the various branches of the armed services and indicating as far as possible, the equivalents of these programs in terms of the subjects generally taught in the secondary schools or the institutions of higher learning. Possibly suggestions will be made concerning the approximate equivalents in terms of credit hours.

The second problem associated with the training of ex-service personnel certainly will be the kind of subject matter that will be made available. Most of the men will return to civilian life still young chronologically but old in experience. They will feel that they have lost several years from their lives, and they will want to get back to making a living as soon as possible. Probably they will have little patience with prerequisite requirements, tightly drawn curricular patterns, or other regulations that might tend to restrict the scope of their educational activities. Many will want vocational training in lieu of a liberal education.

It is at this point that we find our greatest divergence of opinion with respect to postwar education. Yale and Harvard are excellent cases in point. Representatives of these two institutions met a few weeks ago to discuss plans for postwar education but failed to agree on anything except that financial aid from the government must not be permitted to threaten academic control of the postwar policy. As reported by *Time* magazine, Yale's president, Charles Seymour, announced that veterans going to New Haven would not attend Yale

College, but would enroll in an institute of collegiate study, where college life would be adapted to war-weathered students. Summer vacations, dropped for the duration, would be restored because year-round schooling is unprofitable or disastrous. Since Yale is not equipped for vocational training, it will continue to stress the humanities.

Harvard's president, James Bryan Conant, dismissed the notion of teaching the humanities to any considerable portion of the ten million veterans, since returned soldiers will be in a hurry. Harvard will function on an all-year program. Veterans uninterested in or inept at "book learning" may get a year of vocational training leading to industrial jobs.

What will the Oklahoma institutions do? The problem is perhaps greater at the University than elsewhere, or at least it will be greater in those institutions which are committed to the principle that a liberal education is the best preparation not only for making a life but for making a living as well. Be that as it may, the facts will have to be faced realistically, and the needs of the returning servicemen will have to be met.

Another problem facing us squarely is the place that research will play in our future planning. Dean Jones, of the Harvard Graduate School, discussed this problem recently before a meeting of the Deans of Southern Graduate Schools, and my remarks that follow are based in part upon his discussions. The first graduate programs in this country were set up in the early part of the nineteenth century. It was assumed at that time that knowledge is indefinitely extensible in all directions, and each graduate student was expected to extend knowledge somewhat in his own particular field. Any increment to knowledge, however fragmentary, was regarded as worthwhile, and our degrees at the graduate level came to be thought of as essentially research degrees.

What the future is to bring forth in this connection is,

I think, evident from the present trend. During the past several years most of the recipients of degrees from our graduate colleges have not been research workers. For the most part they have been technicians and practitioners. They have completed curricula in the various professions, especially education, and their theses for the most part have been concerned with the clarification and evaluation of existing knowledge rather than the discovery of new facts. We no longer regard research as the primary function of the graduate program. This is perhaps due to the fact that educators are beginning to realize that knowledge cannot be extended indefinitely in all fields by immature minds.

This brings up the question of faculty research. When Gilman organized Johns Hopkins University, research was regarded principally as a function of higher institutions of learning. In recent years research has to a certain extent moved out of academic circles; at least it has appeared elsewhere. Industrial laboratories and research institutes have appeared all over the country, and in these highly specialized agencies it is possible to carry on huge cooperative research projects on a scale unattainable in the average university.

Regimentation and planning have altered somewhat our ideas of intellectual progress through the medium of research. In the minds of some this means that research can be expected virtually to disappear from the campus. I do not think that this will prove to be the case. On the contrary, I believe that the institutions of higher learning may take on increasing importance as agencies of basic research. Regimentation such as is found in the large industrial laboratories may be very effective in arriving at a quick solution to a given problem. However, it is not conducive to the development of ingenuity and originality by the participant in the project.

I do not favor the idea of regimentation or of too much planning by administrators for research in higher institutions.

It seems to me that it would be far better for each individual to pursue the line of his greatest interest and work cooperatively or independently, as seems best, in bringing his program to fruition. In this way the full potentialities of each research worker could be developed, and a large group of highly trained specialists could be made available for the solution of the many unique problems that arise in industrial research.

We have a Research Institute at the University of Oklahoma. It was set up primarily to provide research aid for the smaller southwestern corporations that had not been able, or had not found it expedient, to set up research departments of their own. We have served many of these smaller corporations, but, curiously enough, our greatest contributions have been made to the larger corporations, many of which have developed very fine research laboratories. In most of these instances we have been asked to solve difficult technical problems that could be handled only by some investigator who had spent his life studying some very limited area of science.

It seems to me also that research is an almost indispensable aid to the teaching process. Learning proceeds most satisfactorily when it is a cooperative enterprise, that is, when individuals at different levels are learning together. The teacher and research worker would represent one level of the process, and the student another—all, however, learning together. The inspiration that comes to a teacher through a sustained research program can be translated into enthusiastic teaching and effective leadership.

In the long run, the success of the university, as it strives to become a vital influence in the development of southwestern culture, will depend to a very great extent upon the financial support it is able to obtain from the people. At the moment we are facing what may develop into a financial crisis. You read in the papers last Saturday that the Army Specialized Training Program would be curtailed sharply by April 1, 1944, and the total number of trainees would probably be reduced about 75 percent. The reason for this isn't clear, but some say that the Army may be planning the "big push" onto the continent of Europe in an effort to knock Germany out of the war quickly and that the ASTP personnel will be used as reserves. Last Sunday I received a telegram from the offices of the Eighth Service Command ordering the university to suspend incurring obligations in connection with certain paragraphs of our basic Reserve Officers Training Corps training-unit contracts. How this will affect the University is not entirely clear, but there will be an adverse effect on our budget, you may be sure. The effect won't be felt until next fall, and I think that we will be able to work out of it in good shape, but our long-range financial problem is really a problem.

We need money for many things—buildings, equipment and especially salaries. Our faculty salaries range from $300 to $1,000 a year lower in each rank than those of our neighboring institutions. Until this is remedied, we will continue to have a heavy turnover in personnel—we will be a sort of academic boot camp where young scholars serve an educational apprenticeship. This is a matter of regret, because every time we lose a productive scholar not only do we lose his services but we suffer a disturbance of our group organization until the new arrival finds his or her place in the order.

I do not know how to get more money for the University, and I probably won't have a chance to try, but I suspect that our future depends to a very large extent not only on how well we teach and do research but also on that intangible something that Stewart Harral, the Director of Press Relations in the School of Journalism, calls "public relations."

212

You know as well as I do, our relations with the public have not always been of the best, but I have received a lot of firsthand information during the past two months. We are regarded by a considerable portion of the population of Oklahoma as being indifferent, supercilious, and a bit snobbish. I know that this is not true, and I have cast about a bit in an effort to find an explanation for the belief. I think that the explanation may be somewhat as follows: The University is the educational capstone of the state. Instructors in other institutions would like to be here. Sooner or later the graduates of other institutions come to wish, though this would not be admitted, that they had received a degree from here. Under these conditions there is bound to be a certain amount of resentment and criticism of us. People expect us to be aware of the situation and to show that we are aware of it. Because of this, our difficulties in establishing good relations with the public are increased, but our responsibilities are increased in the same measure.

I will try to make clear what I mean by mentioning some concrete examples of bad public relations and a similar number of good public relations that have been mentioned to me during the past year. The bad ones stem from a very small percentage of the faculty—perhaps only a fraction of 1 per cent, but it is inevitable that they should be more widely publicized than all of our good ones. However, inasmuch as we will never get any more money to develop the university than the people want us to have, it is to our interest to establish the best of relations with the public.

Poor public relations:

1. An instructor walked into a class of forty-five students at the beginning of the last semester and remarked as follows: "There are forty-five of you in here, and we are equipped to handle only twenty-five; this means that the twenty making the lowest grades will be flunked out at an early date."

2. At the beginning of last semester another instructor failed to make a reading assignment in the textbook, though the students had been asked to buy a book costing about four dollars. One rather timid student who did not know what it was all about, asked the instructor for an assignment after several days had gone by, and the instructor replied, "The assignment is pages 1 to 425; if you will be alert as we go along, you will know what to read."

3. An out-of-town visitor arrived at the office of a faculty member at five minutes to five in the afternoon, and his office was locked. The visitor called the faculty member in question and was told brusquely that he would be in his office at a certain time the next morning.

4. A visitor on the campus a few weeks ago drove up to the curb and asked a faculty member where he could find a member of the engineering faculty. He was told, "I don't know."

Good public relations:

1. An instructor met a large class in an overcrowded classroom about a year ago. He apologized to the class for the crowded conditions and said he hoped that it would not interfere too much with the success of the course. He said that he would conduct an extra session each Thursday evening from seven to eight o'clock, or at some other time at their convenience, for the benefit of any students who felt that they were not getting along with their work as well as they had hoped.

2. An instructor in a science department on the campus supplies each student with a mimeographed list of reading assignments covering the entire semester. He announces the first time each class meets that he will be glad to confer with each student concerning the reading and other requirements of the course.

3. A visitor to the campus coming to see our premedical adviser had car trouble and arrived at 5:30 P.M. He called the adviser, explained his predicament, and asked whether it would be possible to have an appointment that evening. The adviser invited him to dinner and talked to him about his son's medical program until late in the evening.

4. Recently a stranger on the campus appeared in the office

214

of a department chairman and asked the whereabouts of an instructor whose office was in another building. The chairman had his secretary take the visitor to the proper office.

As I said at the beginning, we cannot predict the future with certainty in these uncertain times. However, it seems obvious that the questions that I have mentioned will come up in our future planning and that their solution will, to a very great extent, influence educational developments in this area in the next decade.

I realize that these remarks have been rambling. I should like to close by saying that I believe that the university has enormous possibilities for rendering service. It is very young, as great universities go, and essentially an educational frontier where, with adequate financial support, its development will be limited only by the imagination of its faculty. Like many of you, I am not a native of Oklahoma. I came here of my own free will ten years ago because I thought this was a good place. I still think so.

APPENDIX 2

Atomic Energy and Human Relations

(SPEECH DELIVERED TO OKLAHOMA CITY ROTARY CLUB, NOVEMBER 27, 1945)

I was in Washington when I received my invitation to appear here today. The telegram containing the invitation was sent in care of Mike Monroney, Oklahoma City's popular congressman. After accepting the invitation, I had a long talk with Mike, and later I visited the offices of several other members of the Oklahoma delegation to pay my respects and to talk with them briefly about the various problems of the day.

I found that they were all very much interested in atoms—they wanted to talk about the atom—the atomic bomb—and the international implications of atomic energy. Many of them were more than merely interested in these matters. Some seemed a bit frightened about what the future might hold in store for the country and world.

A year ago this would have seemed a bit unusual because, after all, no one has really seen an atom—or felt an atom—or smelled an atom—or touched an atom—or heard an atom. Atoms vary in size, but all are small. The ones in which the congressmen were interested are only about 1/250,000,000 inch in diameter, and most of what they contain is empty space. Each atom consists of a dense central nucleus made up of protons and neutrons surrounded by a vaporous cloud of electrons. The central nucleus, in which the congressmen were most interested, is less than 1/2,000,000,000 inch in diameter. The distance from the nucleus to the outer shell of electrons is approximately 5,000 times the diameter of the nucleus. It might seem a little odd that anything so small should be causing so much commotion in our nation's capital.

216

All substances are made of atoms, and there are 92 different kinds of atoms found in nature. They have been arranged by physicists according to their weight; the lightest is hydrogen, and the heaviest is uranium. All the congressmen were interested in the uranium atom. There was no mention of the other 91. Of course, this interest was occasioned by the fact that only recently we have learned to split the nuclei of uranium atoms with a tremendous release of energy. We announced our success to the world last August, when we obliterated two Japanese cities with two atomic bombs.

I want to discuss with you this afternoon some of the problems that have been brought about by this development. But before doing so I should like to review briefly some of the history associated with the development of atomic power. Sometimes it is possible to interpret the future in the light of the past.

Sir Isaac Newton, the distinguished English scientist, working during the late seventeenth and early eighteenth centuries, discovered many of the fundamental laws of motion and concluded that these laws are applicable to small bodies as well as large ones. He concluded further that everything is made up of tiny particles that were later called atoms. A Russian scientist named Dmitri Mendeleev, later in the eighteenth century, arranged the known atoms according to their atomic weight. Antoine Becquerel, a Frenchman, discovered that uranium gives off invisible radiation and in 1896 announced the existence of radioactivity. Pierre and Marie Curie, French and Polish scientists, respectively, collaborating at the turn of the century, discovered radium and were able to show that radium and uranium, as well as other substances, decompose when radioactive rays are given off. Albert Einstein, a German Jew, from purely mathematical calculations concluded that a substance can be converted

217

into energy so completely that no trace is left. His famous equation, developed in 1905, that the energy in a substance is equal to its mass times the velocity of light squared, was proved correct by developments in the laboratory. Early in the twentieth century Niels Bohr, a Danish physicist, gave us our first basic theory of the structure of the atom; he announced that an atom consists of a nucleus with electrons revolving about it. A bit later Enrico Fermi, an Italian, bombarded uranium atoms with neutrons and produced some new kinds of radioactive atoms. Still later, Lise Meitner, a physicist of German Jewish ancestry, working in Copenhagen with a British scientist named Otto Frisch, demonstrated the splitting of the uranium nucleus into two parts with a release of energy. Bohr, the Danish physicist, was then able to show that the uranium nuclei most easily split were not those of ordinary uranium but of a type known as uranium 235.

Uranium 235 is a very rare material; it occurs in ordinary uranium in the amount of 0.7 percent. However, the great group of scientists assembled from all over the world to work on the atomic-bomb projects in the three American laboratories set up for the purpose found that ordinary uranium could be converted into a substance known as plutonium, which could be exploded atomically just as easily as uranium 235. Plutonium presumably is the material out of which the atomic bomb was made.

I have given you this rather long historical review not because I expect you to remember any details of what I have said but to illustrate one point, namely, that the release of atomic energy has been an international project. Starting back in the seventeenth and eighteenth centuries with the work of Sir Isaac Newton, it was made possible by the cooperation and free interchange of knowledge among scientists of all lands—even Japanese physicists have made a contribution. Now I am not going to tell you in the next breath that I think that this new development that led to the atomic bomb should be made freely available to the scientists of all lands, because I don't know the answer to that one. I only hope that the congressmen in Washington who make the decision will know.

This project of releasing atomic energy represents perhaps the greatest intellectual achievement of mankind. Now it remains to be seen whether we have sufficient intellectual ability to keep from using the results of these labors for the destruction of our civilization. It would seem that if we were intelligent enough to do the one thing we should be clever enough to do the other. That does not necessarily follow, because the social, economic, and political sciences, which deal with human relations, have lagged far behind the natural sciences and technology. I dislike being a pessimist, but I must say frankly that I think that atomic energy has been released about fifty years ahead of its time—or ahead of the time when mankind can use it as a benefaction.

Now let us discuss some of the potentialities of atomic energy. Its destructive possibilities are, of course, apparent. The University lent a young physicist, Francis Dudley Williams, to the project in New Mexico. He has not yet been released to return to the campus for teaching and research, but he did visit us for a few days soon after the war ended. He told some of his colleagues that the scientists who were working on the project had hoped up until the time of the test that they would be able to prove definitely and without any doubt that it is impossible to produce an atomic bomb. They had hoped that their mathematical calculations would prove to be erroneous in some respect. Their calculations were erroneous, to some extent, but not in the way that they had hoped. They underestimated the force of an atomic explosion. Williams had charge of a set of instruments on the day of the test explosion. His instruments were in a concrete pillbox about eight miles from the test area. The instruments were designed to measure the concussion, the light and heat liberated during the explosion. They had been estimated to have sufficient capacity for that purpose.

When the bomb went off, however, the instruments were found to be completely inadequate. They registered full capacity immediately and were useless thereafter. The light and the heat, even at that distance from the explosion, were so great that the scientists were actually terrified, and many of them suffered temporary blindness. Another research worker from our Department of Physics was stationed at the main research plant about two hundred miles from the test area. He reported that, even at that remote position, he could see plainly the intense flash of light that followed the explosion. Many were apprehensive that the experiment had gotten out of control with unpredictable consequences. The tremendous crater produced by the bomb and the obliteration of the steel rack upon which the bomb was suspended are well known to all. When he came to the Norman campus, Williams brought with him samples of desert sand fused into glass. The samples were so radioactive that he had to keep them in a lead case. The first trips into the bombed area were made in tanks lined with lead to protect the investigators from harmful radioactive effects.

The economic possibilities of the development can be illustrated in quite another way. The University of Oklahoma had lent John Niessink Cooper, a young scientist, to a project farther west. At Hanford, Washington, on the Columbia River, the government built a large plant to produce plutonium to be used in the construction of atomic bombs. The plant consisted largely of huge graphite piles into which mixtures of uranium 238 and 235 were inserted. The uranium 235 exploded atomically, and as a result of the process some of the uranium 238 was converted into plutonium and other radioactive materials. Some of these radioactive materials will probably be useful later in the medical profession as a substitute for radium and in industry as a substitute for X rays in the testing of metals of various kinds. However, the main point that I want to stress is this: for every kilogram of plutonium produced—1 kilogram is about 2.4 pounds—the equivalent of 1.5 million kilowatts of electricity was released in the form of heat into the Columbia River. This huge number of kilowatts almost equals the entire capacity of the Grand Coulee system. In this instance, of course, the energy was wasted—merely dissipated into the Columbia River, where it raised the temperature of the river somewhat. However, under different circumstances it might well be put to use as a substitute for energy derived from other sources—from coal, gas, and petroleum products.

One pound of uranium 235 is equivalent in energy to 1,600 tons of coal or 200,000 gallons of gasoline. It can be exploded atomically with a release of 11.4 million kilowatt-hours of energy. This is possible if only 0.1 percent—one atom in a thousand—of the atoms in a pound of uranium—is disintegrated. If all the atoms were exploded, the energy released would be much greater, of course—ten thousand times greater.

Uranium 235 at $9,000 a pound could compete successfully with coal at $6 a ton. At $5,000 a pound it could compete with fuel oil at $0.02 a gallon. At $39,000 a pound it could compete with city gas at $0.5 per 1,000 cubic feet. At $10,000 a pound it could compete with natural gas at $0.25 per 1,000 cubic feet, and at $26,000 a pound it could compete with gasoline at $0.10 a gallon. What this may mean to the future economy of our country when efficient methods of liberating the energy have been developed I will leave to your imagination. The potential benefits to the human race may well be beyond the wildest dreams of most of our people.

Of course there are many technical difficulties involved in the application of atomic energy to industry, but when we consider the distance we have come during the past fifty years, it is easy to believe that these difficulties will be overcome.

The problems that we face are almost terrifying in magnitude. We find ourselves the unwilling custodians of a power capable of unraveling the very fabric of our civilization. It is equally susceptible of development as a tremendous force for the social betterment of all mankind. However, while we have proved its destructive possibilities, its constructive applications are still of a somewhat speculative nature.

Out of it all I believe that certain truths emerge. We should not try to conceal our discovery from the rest of the world. Never in the past have we found a way to suppress or conceal scientific developments. In the earlier days we used to hang, behead, or burn scientists who propounded ideas not to our liking. But science went on. It is hopeless to think that full information concerning the atomic bomb will not be available to all civilized nations within the next very few years. As a matter of fact, the production of an atomic bomb is not beyond the capabilities of any small group of reasonably able physicists.

The basic principles of the bomb are pretty well known, but some of the technical details of the highly effective instrument of destruction perfected for use against Japan are still carefully guarded secrets. Probably most atomic bombs produced independently in the near future would not be as efficient as the ones dropped on Japan, but they would still be efficient enough for considerable destruction and could easily be improved with additional experience. After all, the efficiency of the present uranium bomb is only about 2 to 5 percent, which leaves a considerable margin for development.

While the world's deposits of uranium are not extensive—they are found in Canada, Bohemia, the Belgian Congo, Czechoslovakia, and perhaps Russia—there is a strong possibility that other heavy, relatively unstable elements, such as thorium, may very soon be found useful as sources of atomic energy.

Now in one gigantic convulsion our scientific and technological development has passed so far ahead of our social engineering that we have no choice but to turn our full energies to the control of the forces that we have unleashed. To do this effectively, several changes will have to be made in our thinking. In the first place, our outmoded ideas of time and space as factors in national defense will have to be completely discarded. In the postwar world it will be possible to spend weekends not only in London or the European capitals but in central Asia or Australia and be at work on Monday morning. The entire world will be our neighborhood.

We will need to stop fumbling with respect to a world organization and political integration. We will need to develop an international organization with police powers and a highly efficient secret service of the nature of the FBI to prevent the misuse of atomic energy. This is a necessity of fundamental and immediate importance to our continued existence.

At political and economic levels we will need to discard our old-fashioned ideas of racial distinctions based on color, religion, cultural development, or philosophy. This will be hard for many of us because we cling so tenaciously to our old ideas. But now, when we have one last chance to learn to get along together as neighbors with our very existence hanging in the balance, it is high time for us to come to our senses with respect to such things. The white race must give up its tendency to exploit the so-called backward peoples of other races. Gradually it must give up all forms of political and economic control of other races.

223

Of course, we fear other peoples, other races, but that is because we have never been able to arrive at a mutual understanding. For instance, there is considerable concern about the Russians. The Russians do not think as we do, and this makes us uneasy. The Russians plunge forward impetuously with an idea, while we are inclined to study it carefully as we go along. In a debate the Russians' first reaction is to say no—with emphasis. Later they are likely to lose steam and come to an agreement, whereas the Americans will usually say yes but with qualifications. Russians face their problems realistically and very frankly. They appreciate bluntness and hate hypocrisy. They never whitewash a bad situation or cover up or adopt a Pollyanna attitude. They have no patience with anything but the real article. It is said that the Russian soldiers have no pinup girls. They have a very high regard for science and technology, and they admire intellectual achievement. For this reason it would seem that our best chance at arriving at friendly relations would be through the use of scientists as emissaries of good will. In any event, we have got to learn to get along not only with the Russians but with the peoples of all lands.

From this it follows that the future leadership will be secured from all continents and nations of the world. The future of mankind rests with the peoples of China, India, and Africa, the Pacific Islanders and the Latin Americans, as well as the Occidental group to which we belong. But we must take the lead. After all, science and technology are perfectly capable of producing an abundant living for all of mankind with luxuries for those of great imagination who are able to supply leadership. In the words of Allan Nevins, professor of American History at Columbia University: "The cornucopia is there. Science and technology have provided it. The frail hands of man must learn to tilt it accurately, not for the western world alone, but for Asia, Africa, and Oceana."

Just as the development that has brought about this great world crisis has been based on the cooperation of scientists the world over, so the solution of the problems with which we are faced must be based upon international cooperation—and I do mean international cooperation, because, while it may be necessary to blunt our nationalism a bit and discard racial intolerances, a philosophy of economic and political equality need not mean that nations must be cut to one political or economic pattern or that they must lose their autonomy. To say that the entire world must become capitalistic or communistic or adopt any other political philosophy is ridiculous. The world is large enough for all nations to develop their own social and cultural patterns and their own ways of life, but too small for them to try to impose their ways on others.

However, in the final analysis, "God made of one blood all nations of mankind to dwell on the face of the whole earth." The idea that there is but one human race, which constitutes a single grand family of Mankind, must prevail if the race is to continue.

The Ethical Use of Professional Competence

(SPEECH DELIVERED TO SCHOOL OF BANKING, UNIVERSITY OF WISCONSIN, AUGUST 31, 1956)

First of all, I should like to express my appreciation of the opportunity to be with you this evening and participate in your commencement ceremonies. I bring you greetings from the University of Oklahoma, an institution that has been interested in the profession of banking for many years. I bring you greetings from our faculty, some of whom may regard bankers and banking with mixed emotions, but all of whom have periodic need for the services of your profession. I bring you my own personal greetings and my assurances of respect for your profession. Back at home, with the exception of the University's governing board and the Oklahoma Legislature, I make greater effort to get along with my local bank than with any other agency or institution.

To the members of this class of 1956, I extend my heartiest congratulations and every good wish for successful service in the future.

I congratulate, also, the founders of the School of Banking of the University of Wisconsin who made your fine program possible. From your catalogue I notice that the school was started back in 1945 for the purpose of "providing bankers an opportunity for advanced study and research in banking, economic and monetary problems." I was amazed to note that the school's first enrollment of forty-seven students led, within ten years, to an enrollment of approximately nine hundred. This great growth and development provide concrete evidence of your belief in education as a means of improving the professional services you provide the public.

Your confidence in education apparently has been shared widely by your fellow Americans in all walks of life. Your school was established in the last decade of a century of unprecedented educational development in our country. Between 1850 and 1950 the overall population of our country increased six times, but the enrollment in our colleges and universities increased two hundred times. Dr. Oliver Carmichael, former president of the University of Alabama, has referred to this as "perhaps the most amazing fact in a century of fantastic progress." Our colleges and universities have become vast information factories and reservoirs of knowledge. The knowledge has been acquired through research. It has been classified and made available to increasing numbers of students, and the end is not in sight. Paramount in all of this has been the development of professional education and a high degree of professional specialization in our colleges and universities. A student can attain competence and a degree in almost any profession by following the appropriate curriculum in a university and by passing certain examinations. He may or may not receive an education in the process, but he can become skilled professionally.

This great educational development of the past hundred years can be correlated with an equally overwhelming economic development that occurred during the same period of time. Which of these great developments may be cause and which effect is difficult to establish. Perhaps they can be regarded as parallel developments brought about by aggressive characteristics inherent in the American people. But the correlation exists, and the fact exists that the United States leads all nations in the extent of educational and economic development.

The statistics concerning our economic development

are most impressive. In a speech to the Manufacturers Association of Syracuse in February, 1956, President William P. Tolley, chancellor of Syracuse University, said:

> In the past hundred years we have raised our productivity by more than six times, have reduced our hours of work per week by 40 per cent, and have had a five-fold increase in our standard of living. The battle of agricultural production has been won. Our problem is no longer one of hunger or scant supply, but what to do about production in excess of needs. We have won the battle of production in industry. Even in war time we can have both guns and butter. Problems of distribution continue to haunt us, but even here we are making enormous progress.
>
> The number of American families with an annual income of from $5,000 to $10,000 per year has moved from 8.7 million to 15.7 million in 1955, or from 19% to 32% of all families. This is an 80% increase in five years. Another 7% of the families have incomes of $10,000 or more and this number has increased 90% in the last five years. In 1950, 77% of the families had an income of $5,000 or less; now five years later, only 61% are in this group. Notice, however, that the yardstick is $5,000 or less. By the standards of other nations, this is not a yardstick of poverty but of wealth. Grinding, desperate poverty such as most other people experience every day of the year is largely behind us. To be sure, we shall always have unfilled wants. There will be always people in need. There will always be handicapped and underprivileged. But, looking at American society as a whole, for perhaps the first time in history the great battle against poverty has been won.

There are other statistics that prove this point. Our people constitute collectively less than 6 percent of the world's population but yet have 40 percent of the world's income. Our citizens own over $300 billion in liquid assets—the highest per capita ownership of wealth of any nation. Our per capita income of a little over $1,500 is easily the highest in the world.

But despite the tremendous educational and economic developments of the past century, and the physical comfort that these have brought to us, our people are beset by misgivings and apprehensions for the future. To most of us the future probably seems more uncertain now than in any other time in our history. We live in a highly nervous and unstable world. There are feelings of fear and uncertainty throughout the world. These fears and the recent remarkable increase in church membership in the United States provide evidence that our people sense that something is wrong—that there are questions which are not answered by research or professional knowledge.

The cause of these misgivings is the uncertainty that exists in the minds of nearly all of us about how our vast knowledge of physical things, and the power made possible by this knowledge, will be used in the future affairs of mankind. The spectacular advance in nuclear physics during the past 100 years has made available a source of power undreamed of at the beginning of the period. The almost equally spectacular advances in communications and transportation have reduced the world to the dimensions of a small community, in any part of which any nation ultimately will be able to use the power for destructive or constructive purposes depending upon the attitudes of those in control. The people know that, if the power which we now possess had been available to leaders like Hitler, Mussolini, and Stalin, the results would have been disastrous. They know also that such power will be available to leaders in the future. That they should be a bit nervous under these circumstances is understandable.

In the overall perspective it would seem that man has made far greater progress in solving problems having to do with his physical environment—his world in his universe—than he has made in solving problems that are inherent in him. He has learned a great deal about the various sciences, such as physics, chemistry, geology and biology, and he has devised clever ways of applying this information in securing food, shelter, entertainment, and the conveniences of everyday living. But he has done little toward the solution of problems based on his own emotions and attitudes. While he has learned to control his environment and no longer needs have fear of the elements, he has made little if any progress in learning to control or manage his emotions. In comparison with any field of modern science, individual and social psychology may be said to be in their infancy.

Envy, greed, lust, and malice constitute as great a threat to our welfare today as they did in the stone age—indeed, an even greater threat, because man now has almost unlimited supplies of knowledge and power to use in expressing his attitudes and emotions. The control of emotions and the development of proper attitudes in the use of modern knowledge and power are the principle educational problems of the future. Perhaps they are also the most neglected problems in modern education. I suspect that their significance is not understood by those who work in the professions and industry.

As I view higher education in relation to these problems, it occurs to me that those responsible for its content have stressed subject matter, research, and the development of professional knowhow too much and have not done enough to develop in their students the moral values and ethical attitudes that will be necessary if the fruits of our research laboratories and the products of our professional schools are to be used wisely in human affairs. I suspect that too much attention has been given to information and techniques—far too little to attitudes and values. For this reason it seems to me that graduates of our colleges and universities go out into the professions and the business world with something lacking—an educational gap, so to speak, between professional knowledge on the one hand and professional ethics or morality on the other. In most instances, I believe, the gap is never closed, possibly because those engaged in the professions and in business devote so much attention to what has been called "public relations" and so little attention to the more basic problems of "human relations."

Public relations is, of course, a superficial aspect of human relations, but it is a vastly overrated concept in modern affairs. Too frequently, as Robert Maynard Hutchins once put it, "public relations means trying to find out what the prevailing opinion is before you act and then acting in accordance with it." Or, equally frequently, it means providing preferential treatment or special favors for those who may be in a position to reciprocate later in a professional or business sense.

The concept of human relations, on the other hand, has much deeper significance. This concept has to do with basic behavior of all human beings in relation to each other. Thus, as between individuals, the quality of one's human relations will be determined by the quality of his behavior toward all others in his group, not by his behavior toward a select few.

As between groups, the quality of one group's human relations will be determined by its behavior toward all other groups. The basic problem would seem to be to improve each individual's behavior in relation to all other individuals, and each group's behavior in relation to all other groups.

The ultimate objective—never to be attained, of course—would be ideal individual and group behavior.

There is a science of ideal human behavior—that branch of philosophy known as "ethics." Webster has defined ethics as "a science of moral duty" or, more broadly, "the science

231

of ideal human behavior." Thus ethics, moral law, and ideal human behavior are approximately equivalent. The great disparity between our ethical and moral development as compared with our scientific and economic development, is the barrier that may prevent a wise use of the knowledge and power we now possess. Raymond B. Fosdick summarized the problem well in a speech that he gave in California in 1948: "Unless we can anchor our knowledge to moral purposes, the ultimate result will be dust and ashes—dust and ashes that will bury the hopes and monuments of men beyond recovery. The towering enemy of man is not his science, but his moral inadequacy." More recently, D. B. Steinman expressed the same general idea during a speech at the University of Michigan in May, 1956:

> Civilized man is feeling the strain. There is a weary feeling . . . of having glimpsed in atomic power more of mastery—and of death—than man is ready to face. Perhaps the fear and soul-searching it induces are hopeful signs. The realization grows upon us that the spiritual ideal has ceased to be a luxury and has become an absolute necessity. Today, in a literal sense never before so apparent, the moral law has become the law of survival."

I am sure that all of this seems a bit theoretical and that many very practical questions will emerge in your thinking. What is moral law? What is ideal human behavior? What are proper attitudes? How can a single individual hope to make use of these concepts in such a way that the international situation may be improved? These are good questions that each individual must answer for himself, presumably after considerable soul-searching.

It is difficult to define ethics or ideal human behavior, because, as I pointed out in the talk given before the American College of Life Underwriters a year ago, ideas of ethical behavior, like styles and fashions, seem to have changed through the ages and are still changing.

Concepts of ethics have varied and still vary geographically, in accordance with the customs and mores of the different kinds of people who inhabit the earth. They vary even among individuals in a community, in accordance with the past experiences of each individual.

Thus the use of cosmetics was considered ethical, though perhaps a bit misleading, in the ancient Egyptian world. It was considered immoral in early American history and today is regarded as a proper deception in most parts of the world.

Witch burning is still a moral custom in certain parts of the world, and was accepted as a desirable moral practice during the early history of some of our New England states.

The practice of charging interest for money loaned has been considered at various times and in various places as both moral and immoral. Currently it is considered a desirable business practice in our own country but not so in Soviet Russia.

In ancient Greece there was even some confusion in regard to the morality of truthfulness. Plato in one of his dialogues (the third book of *The Republic*) gave the privilege of lying to the rulers of the state but made it a criminal offense for the common people not to tell the truth. There is some tendency for this bit of ancient philosophy to persist in modern politics.

All of this is confusing, and the result is that many people today think of ideal human behavior only in terms of how other people should behave. Where can we find a reliable guide to moral law and human behavior? Is there anywhere a basic truth—a guide to living—something concisely stated and with general historical acceptance? Wide acceptance is important, because no rule or precept has value by itself. It is the wide agreement of people upon a concept that makes it a value.

I looked into this matter a few years ago when I was invited to make a talk on ethics before a group of lawyers. I found that our modern ideas of ethics and moral law have developed historically as a part of religious thought. According to Lewis Browne's *The World's Great Scriptures,* Confucius taught moral law as a part of religion. He said: "Is there one maxim which ought to be acted upon throughout one's whole life? Surely it is a maxim of loving-kindness: Do not unto others what you would not have them do unto you." To my very great interest I found that this same admonition appears also in writings of Brahaminism, Buddhism, Taoism, Zoroastrianism, Islam, Judaism, and Christianity.

There are distinctions of phrasing, but no difference in meaning. The ancient Jewish writer in the Talmud admonished: "What is hateful to you, do not unto your fellow men. That is the entire law: all the rest is commentary." In the New Testament a more positive approach is taken: "All things whatsoever ye would that men should do unto you, do ye even also unto them: For this is the law and the prophets." In modern usage we say simply, "Do unto others as you would have others do unto you," and call it the Golden Rule. Here, very tersely stated, is a principle that has found almost universal acceptance and upon which all religious philosophers have agreed. The individual who understands this concept, and its implications, needs no other guide to living, for, as the ancient Jewish writer put it in the Talmud, "This is the entire law. All else is commentary."

It is inevitable, of course, that the practical-minded man will ask, "What place do ethics and moral law have in the highly competitive existence which faces professional personnel in 1956?" The practical man will point out that competition has been traditional in our American way of life. Rugged individualism has made our country strong. How can one observe the Golden Rule and still be practical? Must competition be eliminated? Must the desire of the individual to get along in the world be stifled?

Ethical living and the observance of the Golden Rule do not eliminate competition or the desire to get ahead in the world. The rule merely provides that such competition and effort to get ahead will be based entirely upon one's ability, efficiency, and willingness to exert honest effort. It is the purpose of professional training to develop one's ability, to increase his efficiency, and to help him see the value of honest effort. It is the purpose of moral law to ensure that trickery or subterfuge of any kind is not used in one's efforts to get ahead. A man's success should be *determined* by his ability, efficiency, and industry. His success should be *measured* by the quality of the service that he renders and the integrity of his relations with his associates.

The moral quality of any group of people, from community to nation, from bankers to savings and loan executives, is determined by the total moral and ethical qualities of all the individuals included in the group. Each individual is responsible for his contribution. An unfortunate trend in our own country is the increasing tendency of many of our citizens to think and talk in terms of the rights and privileges of the individual in a democratic society, with a lessening inclination to stress the responsibility of the individual. I should like to emphasize that it is the responsibility of the individual, rather than his rights and privileges, that gives him his strength, and gives democracy its strength. Our failure to meet squarely our individual responsibilities for the maintenance of moral law may be a serious factor in the unrest, tension, and uncertainty of modern times.

Perhaps many who accept this idea in principle may

wonder how it can work in practice. Exactly how can an individual use his initiative in promoting better ethical behavior for himself and for his group?

His first step is to reject the idea that he has acquired his education and his professional competence in order to gain an advantage over his fellow men, to control them or exploit them for reasons of personal gain. He should concentrate on the idea of rendering superior service to them. If he will do this, the personal gain will take care of itself without further thought on his part.

He should take vigorous initiative in the rigorous observance of the established ethics of his profession, or, if his profession has not established a code of ethics, he should provide leadership in urging the need for a code and in helping develop it.

He should assume continuing responsibility for studying and refining the ethical procedures that may have been established and accepted by his associates in his profession and community. He should accept the responsibility of helping bring about new and improved ethical procedures for use in his profession. Because change is inevitable, ideas of ethical behavior must change, and the change will be either for better or for worse. Thus practices considered completely acceptable in a profession at one time may prove to be completely unacceptable under the changed conditions of a later period. The same situation will exist in any community. It is the responsibility of the individual to use his influence to the end that any change in the group attitudes toward ethical behavior will result in improved attitudes.

In practical application it will be difficult, of course, to judge and choose among different courses of action when dealing with one's associates, but the infallible guide will always be the Golden Rule. When there may be occasional doubts about the course of action in dealing with others, the individual will find it safe to imagine that the situation is reversed and then ask himself the question, "Would I consider the contemplated action to be reasonable and just?" If an honest affirmative answer can be given, there will be no need for further doubt. The individual will have observed moral law to the best of his ability.

In the insurance profession the American College of Life Underwriters has an interesting charge that it has incorporated into an agreement with the Chartered Life Underwriters. It reads: "I shall, in the light of all the circumstances surrounding my client, which I shall make every conscientious effort to ascertain and to understand, give him that service which, had I been in the same circumstances, I would have applied to myself."

A slight change in this charge would produce a personal code that would be useful to all, namely, "I shall, in the light of all circumstances surrounding those with whom I live, which I shall make every conscientious effort to ascertain and to understand, give them that consideration and treatment which, had I been in the same circumstances, I would have applied to myself."

It would be difficult to devise a personal code more basically sound, more conducive to better attitudes and values, or more in keeping with the wisdom that has come to us from the past. It would be impossible to provide a more fitting supplement to professional education.

A Note on Sources

Quotations credited to Robert Maynard Hutchins were taken from a copy of a speech that he gave at a trustee-faculty dinner at the South Shore Country Club in Chicago, January 12, 1944.

Quotations credited to Charles Dollard, Walter A. Jessup, Otis D. Coffman, W. Allen Wallace, and William P. Tolly were taken from a talk that I gave on the tenth anniversary of my presidency of the University of Oklahoma. At that time I had in my possession printed copies of speeches these individuals had made and other materials reporting their words. These materials were lost after I retired from the presidency of the University.

The quotations credited to Clark Kerr are taken from his *The Uses of the University* (Cambridge, Mass.: Harvard University Press, 1963), chap. 1.

Quotations credited to Harold Stokes are from his *The American College President* (New York, Harper & Brothers, 1959), page 20.

Quotations credited to Herman B. Wells are from his speech "How to Succeed as a University President Without Really Trying," published in the *Educational Record* (Summer, 1944), p. 241.

Index

241

244

Letters to Bill

designed by Bill Cason, was set by the University of Oklahoma Press in 12-point Garamond and printed offset on 60-pound Glatfelter Hi-Bulk, a permanized sheet, with presswork by Cushing-Malloy, Inc. and binding by John H. Dekker and Sons, Inc.